MW00851757

ACOUSTIC GUITAR GUIDES

SONGWRITING AND THE GUITAR

STRING LETTER PUBLISHING

Publisher: David A. Lusterman

Editor: Jeffrey Pepper Rodgers

Designer: Gary Cribb

Production Coordinator: Christi Payne

Marketing Manager: Jen Fujimoto

Production Director: Ellen Richman

Cover photographs: Dick Boak, Jana Leon, John Patrick Salisbury, and Michael Wilson.

Interior photographs: Cecilia Van Hollen, pp. 8, 55; Jack Vartoogian, p. 11; courtesy of C.F. Martin and Co., p. 17; Henry Diltz, pp. 14, 27; Jay Blakesberg, pp. 19, 29; Mickey Krakowski, p. 24; Michael Wilson, p. 32; Jana Leon, pp. 37, 39; Scott Blum, pp. 72, 73.

© 2000 by String Letter Publishing, Inc.

David A. Lusterman, Publisher

ISBN 1-890490-28-8

Printed in the United States of America.

All rights reserved. This book was produced by String Letter Publishing, Inc.

PO Box 767, San Anselmo, California 94979-0767

(415) 485-6946; www.acousticguitar.com

Library of Congress Cataloging-in-Publication Data

Songwriting and the guitar.

      p. cm — (Acoustic guitar guides)

   ISBN 1-890490-28-8

    1. Guitar—Instruction and study. 2. Popular music—Writing and publishing. I. Series.

MT580 .S67 2000

787.87′193—dc21

                                      00-032233

STRING LETTER PUBLISHING

contents

introduction

The right guitar for songwriting, says Don McLean, should "give you the feeling of Superman when he emerges from a phone booth with his cape flowing." In David Wilcox's estimation, it is the guitar that knows the song; the writer simply listens and follows. For Patty Larkin, experimenting with alternate guitar tunings provides a way to bypass the analytical mind, because "I want to be surprised by what I play. I don't want to think too much." No matter what the style of music or the personality of the artist, the relationship between a songwriter and the guitar is intense, mysterious, and critical to writing a successful song. That relationship is the subject of this book.

Songwriting and the Guitar offers guidance and inspiration to guitar-playing songwriters in several forms. In the first section, In Their Own Words, you'll hear nine of today's best songwriters describe their creative processes—how they get ideas, how they work with (or without) their guitars, how they use various tools and techniques (alternate tunings, capos, chord theory, tape recorders) in the pursuit of a great song. Then, in Workshops, you'll find in-depth, thoughtful advice from seasoned songwriters/teachers on finding inspiration and then polishing your melodies, lyrics, and chord progressions until they shine. The final section, Tools and Resources, offers tips on buying the right guitar, using a capo, and working with a tape or digital recorder as you write. Plus, you'll find a list of 25 alternate tunings, along with examples of songs that use them, that provides a great starting point for exploring this whole new approach to the instrument and to songwriting itself.

In any artistic pursuit, the trick is to keep growing, to challenge yourself and to break out of familiar habits and patterns. Make use of the wisdom and encouragement offered by the songwriters in this book to fuel your quest for words and music that really *sing*.

Jeffrey Pepper Rodgers
Editor

about the authors

JAMIE ANDERSON

Jamie Anderson is a contemporary folk singer-songwriter who teaches songwriting at Duke University as well as other music classes and workshops. Since the late '80s she has toured all over the U.S., appearing at hundreds of venues, including folk and women's music festivals. While she's known for demented songs like "When Cats Take Over the World," she also delves into a range of more serious topics. Her newest recording is *Drive All Night*. Anderson lives in Durham, North Carolina, with her partner and their two enormous felines, who persist in trying to collect royalties for the cat song.

STEPHEN DICK

Guitarist/composer Stephen Dick lives in the Los Angeles area, where he leads the flamenco/jazz trio Mojacar. He studied theory and composition at the New England Conservatory of Music and at San Francisco State University with Pulitzer Prize–winning composers William Thomas McKinley and Wayne Peterson. Dick's compositions for solo guitar have received awards and have been published in Europe and the U.S.

DAVID HAMBURGER

David Hamburger is a guitarist, teacher, and writer who lives in Brooklyn, New York. He has toured with Salamander Crossing and Five Chinese Brothers and appeared on recent recordings by Chuck Brodsky and the Kennedys. A regular instructor at the National Guitar Summer Workshop, Hamburger has written three instruction books, including *The Dobro Workbook*. His latest solo recording is *Indigo Rose,* on Chester Records (www.songs.com).

JAMES JENSEN

James Jensen has been a frequent contributor to *Acoustic Guitar* magazine over the years, interviewing players such as Michael Hedges, Jorma Kaukonen, David Wilcox, and Bruce Cockburn. He currently divides his time between Acoustic Music Resource (a catalog and Web site for instrumental acoustic guitar CDs, tapes, and books) and Solid Air Records (a label featuring such players as Laurence Juber, Doug Smith, John Jorgenson, Preston Reed, and David Cullen), allowing him to stay close to his lifelong passion for acoustic guitar.

RICHARD JOHNSTON

Richard Johnston is a luthier, stringed-instrument repairman, and co-owner of Gryphon Stringed Instruments in Palo Alto, California. He is also coauthor, with Jim Washburn, of the book *Martin Guitars: An Illustrated Celebration of America's Premier Guitarmaker* (Rodale Press). Johnston has been writing for *Acoustic Guitar* magazine since its inception in 1990 and has been a contributing editor since 1995. He has written definitive historical articles on a wide variety of guitars, including vintage flattops, archtops, dreadnoughts, 12-frets, and the Gibson J-200.

HENRY KAISER

California-based musician Henry Kaiser is widely recognized as one of the most creative and innovative guitarists, improvisers, and producers in the fields of rock, jazz, and experimental music. He has appeared on more than 175 albums, and he performs frequently throughout the U.S., Europe, and Japan. A restless collaborator who constantly seeks the most diverse and personally challenging contexts for his music, Kaiser has played with Herbie Hancock, Richard Thompson, David Lindley, Jerry Garcia, Cecil Taylor, D'Gary, Terry Riley, Sonny Sharrock, Derek Bailey, and Bill Frisell.

PATTY LARKIN

After attending college in Oregon, singer-songwriter Patty Larkin headed to the Berklee College of Music in Boston. She honed her performance skills in the subways and the streets and fronted a succession of bands—rock bands, jug bands, Celtic bands—before embarking on a solo career. She has since recorded nine albums of incisive original songs, including *Perishable Fruit* (High Street/Windham Hill 1997), the live collection *A Gogo* (Vanguard 1999), and *Regrooving the Dream* (Vanguard 2000).

DON McLEAN

Don McLean is one of the most popular singer-songwriters of the last three decades. He has nearly 30 albums currently in print, and he tours frequently in the United States and around the world. McLean's current projects include a new recording of originals, a children's album, a Marty Robbins tribute, and the PBS special *Don McLean: Starry, Starry Night* with guests Nanci Griffith and Garth Brooks. In honor of the 30th anniversary of "American Pie," the Martin Guitar Co. created a signature guitar called the Don McLean D-40 DM. President Clinton invited McLean to sing at the Lincoln Memorial to celebrate the new millennium, and McLean was also honored at a Founders' Dinner at the White House for people who have influenced the 20th century.

ELIZABETH PAPAPETROU

Elizabeth Papapetrou is a singer-songwriter, guitarist, and recording engineer who also designs Web pages and runs a Web resource called Motherheart (www.motherheart.org). Originally from the U.K. and now living in Florida, she has been writing for music magazines for more than 17 years.

JEFFREY PEPPER RODGERS

Jeffrey Pepper Rodgers is the founding editor of *Acoustic Guitar* magazine and has been writing extensively on the acoustic music scene since 1989. His profile of Joni Mitchell's guitar and lyrical craft appears in the book *The Joni Mitchell Companion* (Schirmer), and his interview with Dave Matthews and Tim Reynolds is included in their *Live at Luther College* songbook (Cherry Lane). Rodgers' first book, *Rock Troubadours,* will be published by String Letter Publishing in late 2000. A guitarist and singer, he has been putting words and music together since he was a teenager, and his all-acoustic, all-original homegrown CD, *Traveling Songs,* can be sampled at www.jeffreypepperrodgers.com.

STEVE SESKIN

Steve Seskin is a versatile songwriter whose songs have been covered by artists as diverse as Alabama, Waylon Jennings, John Michael Montgomery, Peter Frampton, Paul Young, and Delbert McClinton. Seskin also maintains an active performing career around his home base of northern California and at festivals and acoustic venues throughout the United States and Canada. In recent years his festival appearances have included the Kerrville Folk Festival, Rocky Mountain Folks Fest, Vancouver Folk Festival, and Napa Valley Music Festival. Seskin is also an active lecturer and songwriting teacher for the Northern California Songwriters Association, Nashville Songwriters Association International, and San Francisco State University.

SAM SHABER

Based in New York City, Sam Shaber is a graduate of Cornell University and a touring singer-songwriter with three critically acclaimed albums out on her own label, Brown Chair Records. Her latest release, 1999's *perfecT,* was voted number 7 out of 1,800 titles for Best Independent CD of 1999 on CDBaby.com. She has also been published in *Musician, Performing Songwriter, Home Recording,* and other national magazines. She can be found on the Web at www.samshaber.com.

SIMONE SOLONDZ

Simone Solondz took her first guitar lesson when she was a junior at the University of Pennsylvania in Philadelphia. She began working at *Acoustic Guitar* magazine in 1991 and became the editor in 2000. Her songwriter interviews for the magazine have included David Crosby, Gillian Welch and David Rawlings, Jonatha Brooke, Iris DeMent, and Jay Farrar of Son Volt.

GARY TALLEY

Gary Talley was the original lead guitar player for the '60s group the Box Tops, who reunited in 1997 and are touring again. He works as a guitar teacher and session musician in Nashville and has published a video and book called *Guitar Playing for Songwriters*. He has recorded with such artists as Willie Nelson, Tammy Wynette, Waylon Jennings, and Billy Preston. His songs have been recorded by the Box Tops, Keith Whitley, James Cotton, and others.

PAUL ZOLLO

Paul Zollo is a songwriter, author, and music journalist. His most recent book is *Songwriters on Songwriting, Expanded Edition.* As a songwriter, Zollo has collaborated with a wide range of artists, from Darryl Purpose to Steve Allen. Zollo's first solo album, released in August 2000 by Windy Apple Records, features a duet with Art Garfunkel. Presently the managing editor of *Performing Songwriter* magazine, Zollo has written for *SongTalk, Musician, Acoustic Guitar,* and other publications. He's also written liner notes for the CD boxed set *Paul Simon 1964–1993, The Best of Laura Nyro: Stoned Soul Picnic,* and other releases.

Waiting for a Miracle

Jeffrey Pepper Rodgers

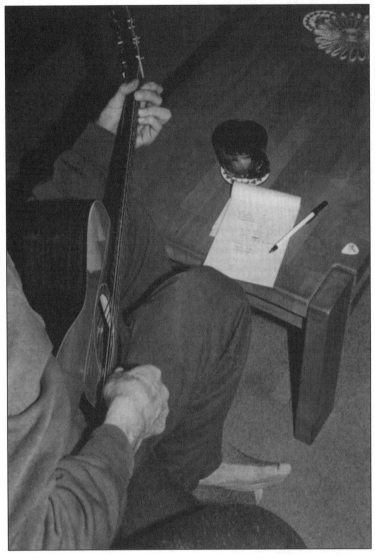

You don't know my songs. Well, some of you out there have heard them—friends and family, friends of friends, scattered strangers and barflies and Web surfers—but that circle is pretty small. Like every other writer, I hope more of you will have a chance to hear my songs someday, but that hope alone doesn't adequately explain why I'm sitting here on yet another night with my guitar in hand, searching for a melody, for why I've been doing this regularly for the last 20 years. The odds of my songs reaching you are too slim.

So this songwriting urge isn't just a matter of trying to reach the masses, and I certainly can't justify my efforts in terms of pots of gold or the proverbial catapult to stardom (if I *did,* I should be carted off immediately to the Garth Brooks Institute for the Commercially Impaired). But neither is songwriting simply a personal journey, a therapy or a party for one. The truth lies somewhere between those two extremes. A songwriter at work sits in pitch darkness, longing for light and knowledge of the surroundings. Every song created is a flare shot into the sky—some bathe the ground in brilliant light, others sputter and die. With each song's burst, the writer looks eagerly around to see if anyone is sitting nearby, listening, illuminated and warmed by the light.

My guitar and I enter a curious sort of partnership in writing a song. On the one hand, it has always been an essential vehicle and guide in this process—the place where the first sparks fly, where a harmonic idea or texture or rhythm meets steel and rings into life. The guitar is where I go searching, ambling around the fingerboard, turning over rocks and kicking up leaves; and when an idea appears, the guitar is the place where I lock onto that idea, maniacally playing it over and over until I fully understand its implications. (The image comes to mind of Jack Nicholson in *The Shining,* typing "All work and no play makes Jack a dull boy" in an endless loop.) When I'm writing, my guitar is at its most magical, seized with spirit and possibility.

On the other hand, the guitar can't be left to its own devices: it chains the melody if I'm not careful. When I listen back to my early songs, on one after another I hear the melody lumbering along precisely on the root of each chord, totally restricted by the chord progression that came first. The melody is like a dog being dragged around on a leash by an overzealous trainer: Heel, heel. *Heel.* Sit! What the guitar should really do in the writing process, I think, is lead the pup to a nice open field, then turn him loose and watch him romp around.

Lots of guitar players are altering their tunings these days to suggest new textures and progressions, but I find that this tinkering can create as many traps as opportunities. A guitar in an unfamiliar open tuning begs you to play certain patterns, to let the open strings vibrate freely into your chest. The effect can be so intoxicating that it's easy to forget that a compositional sensibility has to take charge, that a wash of sound isn't enough.

Tonight, like many recent nights, my guitar resides in dropped-D tuning, a small deviation from standard tuning that opens things up just the right amount for me. I love that little bit of extra range, but I'm still wary of that resonant open D on the sixth string, which always tries to seduce me into the key of D and hates to let me go. Sometimes I'm happy to oblige, but lately I've been writing songs in dropped-D in all kinds of other keys—G, C, F♯, even E♭—and thriving on the challenge and its accompanying burst of new ideas. It forces me to direct the tune very consciously, rather than taking the path of least resistance and letting the guitar do all the work (though it's worth noting that for some gifted songwriters, David Wilcox for example, letting the guitar do all the work is exactly their aim).

An even better way to unchain the melody from the guitar is to leave the guitar behind and come back to it later. Driving, walking, playing my hand drums—I've found all of these to be liberating ways to write. Often the quickest route to that elusive thing called the singable melody is just to sing; how can you sing something that *isn't* singable? An activity like walking particularly seems to set my writing wheels in motion—the rhythm, the distractions of bird calls or car horns, the freedom from purely mental toil and the blank page. And I find that if I choose to fill in chords later (although recently I've been inclined to leave them out, using only percussion and bass), the bare melody most often wants only the most rudimentary chords. There's a moral to that story: *Singable,* it seems, means *simple.* Sometimes it takes forever to grasp the most basic lessons.

It's also true, of course, that the simplest, most singable song is not necessarily the best song. An eminently singable, stick-in-the-eardrum song could as easily be cloying and annoying as it could be timeless and transcendent; the same is true of a hard-to-follow, harmonically adventurous song. Everything depends on the writer's touch. Some writers—Neil Young and John Prine come to mind—manage to find all the complexity and shades of meaning in the world inside a three-chord form. Others—Donald Fagen, Paul Simon—need a wide harmonic vocabulary to get their points across. And the most versatile writers—Paul Simon again—need to have that vocabulary available but know when to ignore it. Think of *Graceland,* which hardly strays from I–IV–V harmonies. The complexity lies elsewhere—in the drum interplay, in the flashing juxtapositions in the lyrics.

But back to the couch and my guitar, where I've got a nibble—a twist of melody and a circle of chords that seems promising. Already, words are coming too—in unconnected nonsense phrases, mostly. Or *are* they nonsense? Should I ignore them, or are they trying to tell me something about what this melody means? If this melody lives for a long time before I write "real" lyrics, and I sing the nonsense lyrics over and over in Nicholson fashion, there's a danger that the nonsense will stick permanently to this song.

I'm trying to guess what this melody wants to be about, but I don't get a clear signal. Maybe this tune will stay wordless for a while, waiting for the right lyrical inspiration to sweep it off its feet. That's OK with me, but I'm a little anxious about how slowly the words are coming: how different this is from when I write in a state of loneliness, longing, pain, or frustration—every singer-songwriter's best friends!—and the words come in a flood. I've been in a period of relative contentment and stability lately, roughly corresponding to a lull in completed songs, and I can't help wondering: Do I have to be down in the dumps to find my muse?

No, I don't think so. The dumps can be perversely inspiring, it's true—and songwriting can be good therapy—but other mental conditions can be equally productive. You might just have to push a little more to get rolling. Recently, I had a bouncy little tune for which I couldn't find lyrics for the longest time. Finally, I played the changes and sang the nonsense lines to my brother, my music partner, and asked him what he thought the song should be about. Without missing a beat, he said, "Write about what it's like to be a dog." Half an hour later, the song was complete, definitely a lighthearted ditty, but as quick and sure and true as any of my howls from the darkness (and a lot more popular at gigs).

A more stable period, when you are less absorbed with your own problems, can be a good time to explore in song the world outside your navel and your diary: to experiment with writing in character, to set a poem to music, to stretch beyond your own experience. One of the greatest bursts of writing I've ever had occurred when I was composing the songs for a musical—a period in which I was forced to write in the voices of several characters with radically different viewpoints—and I had firm, continual deadlines. Even though I haven't been in a similar situation since, I have found it constructive to simulate those kinds of pressures. I've looked over my band's set lists, for instance, and thought, "I should write a percussion-oriented tune to balance out those guitar-heavy ballads," or, "We need some more short songs," or, "I should write another tune in third person." The next gig becomes the deadline, and the songs do tend to arrive on time.

I used to think that writing songs in character was a different process from writing songs from your own experience. But recent conversations with a few masters of both types of writing (Greg Brown, Suzanne Vega) have clarified for me that there should be no distinction between the two: A personal song needs to look beyond your own experience to move your audience, and a character you're evoking has to relate somehow to your own experience in order to ring true. These are two sides of the same coin. The goal of music is communication, and what matters is whether you get there, not how you get there.

In my years as a music journalist and editor of *Acoustic Guitar* magazine, I've been fortunate enough to be able to meet some of my favorite songwriters and ask them to illuminate how they work, why they work, what this whole creative enterprise means to them. Their answers—some of which are included in these pages—have inspired and surprised me, pointing in intriguing directions that I may have never explored or even considered. But the one thing these conversations haven't done is map out a Complete Songwriting Method, with nicely laid-out rules and regulations and step-by-step instructions. Clearly, there aren't any hard-and-fast rules for the writing business. Even if one individual has a few useful rules, those rules are likely to contradict the personal rules of another, equally good writer. We listen to artists speak about their art to take a peek behind the scenes, to see if their method or madness offers any lessons for our own. In other words, we listen to them in interviews for the same reasons we listen to their songs.

Which leaves me here where I started, with a song stirring but still incomplete. Lots of work lies ahead—as much as we hope it will, this process doesn't get any easier. The way I see it, there's only one absolute rule of writing: The songs that we should write are the ones that we *need* to write. And the songs that the audience responds to are the ones that they *need* to hear. All we can do is try to listen closely, write what's necessary and leave out what's not, and sing as clearly as we can.

James Taylor

It's hard to imagine what the term *singer-songwriter* might mean today without the music of James Taylor. From the reflective ballads that reached back to his rural North Carolina childhood to his sophisticated pop-folk songs of the '70s, '80s, and '90s, Taylor has melded thoughtful songwriting with distinctive fingerstyle guitar to form a sound that has inspired several generations of musicians. In a conversation with Jeffrey Pepper Rodgers, he talked about the role of his guitar in the writing process.

How has the way you use your instrument as a writing tool changed over the years?

TAYLOR When I started writing songs, I wrote with guitar and that was it. The songs were written to be played on guitar and sung by a single voice. But then, working with the band, you begin to write more anticipating what the band is going to sound like . . . .

[Even now] there are very few songs that I don't write on guitar. The things that I write on keyboard are even more primitive than the stuff I write on guitar. Some stuff I write a cappella—riding down the road with a tape recorder in an automobile. . . . Writing that way without any accompaniment is interesting; that's a good thing for me to do because it frees me up from the elementary guitar style that I work with.

What are some examples of songs you wrote that way?

TAYLOR "Shed a Little Light" was written without a guitar. "Oh Brother." "Slap Leather."

You've said that your songs are more centered around chord progressions than around melodies. How conscious are you of the theoretical basis of your chords? Do you work them out by feel, or do you think about chord degrees?

TAYLOR Not necessarily chord degrees, but progressions and tone leading and that sort of stuff. It's not that I'm thinking about them—it's just that I have a very clear and very traditional sense of music [based on] church music, Anglican hymns, Christmas carols, that's basically it. Show tunes to a certain extent.

Some of your progressions draw on almost a jazz vocabulary—not that the songs sound like jazz per se, but they're not quite like folk either.

TAYLOR Yeah, but what would you call Joseph Spence? He's definitely a folk musician because he's not schooled. . . . I think that [he played] Anglican church music too. I was amazed to hear him when I was learning to play guitar. He and Ry Cooder very much influenced me.

My music doesn't sound like jazz to me. There are some simple jazz chords—some 13ths and augmented fifths, I play a lot of major sevenths and plus twos—but really a limited jazz vocabulary, for sure, and also very low on the neck, and usually keeping to the root of the chord in the bass. So it's not jazz, and it's not really folk. It's not really church music either, and it has evolved in the context of popular music. It has been informed a lot by the Beatles, a lot by country music, folk music, and a lot of soul music, black music, that I was exposed to.

What I mean to say is that there's a simple vocabulary of chords that I have, and I also have a four-finger picking style that tends to make things very cyclical. I tend to write songs that establish a kind of chordal cycle, and I'll try to fit a melody and lyric into that. More accurately, hopefully, it's a matter of a melody and a lyric happening within that little wheel.

David Wilcox told me that one of the lessons he learned from your music is not to make the melody note the root of the chord, but a more interesting note in the chord. Are you conscious of that quality or does it just happen in your music?

TAYLOR I'm sure it just happens.

My range is sort of a low tenor, and I'm most comfortable in D or E. I feel like those are my keys—I don't know exactly what that means, of course, because you can put the melody wherever you want in the inversion of the chord. Miles Davis once said to me, "D is your key, James." He said very little else to me. He was very encouraging to me, actually, by his standards. But at any rate, he was right.

I wish I had a higher voice, because I feel as though the open guitar from low E to high E is an interesting range. It's not arbitrarily chosen; that's where the guitar really sounds good, and it's a nice range to hear things in, too. It's nice to be able to put your voice well up above that, like in a good, honest tenor, so that you can sing in F, say, and really get those notes. It puts you high above [the guitar], and I like music that's really opened up, that has wide, very open inversions. It really implies a lot of the overtones, it's very rich, you don't have to use a lot of stuff, and you sort of suggest a lot of notes.

I think that's why I stay down the neck, because basically I play guitar as an accompanying instrument, and just basically get a wheel rolling and then hop on the thing and try to ride it. It's nice to be up high enough that you're not tangled up in it.

Are you playing mostly in standard tuning and then just moving the capo around?

TAYLOR Yes. Sometimes I use a G tuning, very infrequently, and there are a number of tunes where I drop the E down to a D, but that's about it.

When you are playing in E, for instance, would you use a capo on the fourth fret and then play open-C fingerings?

TAYLOR I like playing in D so much that to play in E I'm more apt to put a capo on the second fret and to play a D fingering.

In a couple of songs I actually modulate by shifting the capo. In "Your Smiling Face" it happens three times. The song starts in F♯ and then moves up to G♯ and then up to A♯.

Aside from the way your voice feels in different keys, do you think the way a guitar is constructed leads you to a certain key?

TAYLOR To me, it's E, A, and D, or G and C—those are the keys that I play in. A and D are the same for me; they have the same kind of tonal quality to them, and the same with G and C. I'm led there. You see, I haven't made that sort of chromatic leap with the guitar where I can play in any key. I'm an open, standard guitar player with folk, blues, and country roots who likes to play in those keys that give you good access to open notes.

Richard Thompson

Since joining Fairport Convention in 1967, at the age of 17, Richard Thompson has been creating some of the most challenging, vital, and original music in the folk and rock world. As a musician, he's a triple threat: a sharp songwriter, an innovative electric guitarist, and an equally powerful and revered stylist on acoustic guitar. In this conversation with fellow musician Henry Kaiser, Thompson offers a glimpse into his guitar and song craft.

When it's time to write songs, what do you do?

THOMPSON I go to the "office." I'll find a place. It depends which country I'm in and whatever. I'll borrow someone's house or I'll find a workplace where I can go and do office hours. It varies. The earlier in the morning that I can start, the better.

How many hours do you spend each day?

THOMPSON On average, eight.

Will you do this for a week or two at a time?

THOMPSON A week or two is OK, but it's really just getting started. I'd rather do it in months.

Is your guitar in your hands a lot?

THOMPSON Not as much as you might think. I do a lot of writing in my head. I'll refer to the guitar.

Do you take notes? Draw pictures?

THOMPSON I don't do a lot of pictures. I do a lot of drafts, unless it's going well. Some get written in five minutes straight down the line. But that's usually when I'm desperately trying to finish something else. You know, you work desperately hard at one thing, and then the other things just fly. The first thing never gets written; meanwhile you get six other songs that are actually pretty good.

Music first? Lyrics first?

THOMPSON Doesn't matter. Whatever.

You can sit down and do either from scratch with a blank slate?

THOMPSON With difficulty; I don't find it easy at all. It's discipline. The more I do it, the better it gets, the easier it gets. It's the rusty faucet that is hard to get turned on. It takes me a couple of days to get back in to a stride. Dickens used to say it took him a week to get back into writing after he took a gap.

A lot of your songs have strong characters in them.

THOMPSON If you write songs with weak characters, people aren't really going to remember them.

Where do the characters come from?

THOMPSON I don't know. Fantasy. They're fictional characters. I suppose I like to over-draw characters. I'm a Dickens fan. I don't deal in reality. The characters can be totally larger than life. I think there's a reason why characters in songs are larger than life, generally speaking. It is to make them more memorable.

Your arrangements of songs for solo acoustic guitar and voice have become much more complex and daring over the years. What are you striving for in your guitar parts?

THOMPSON I'm definitely trying to amuse myself. I'm trying to push myself to do more, technically. Also, it's a constant battle to try to make an acoustic guitar bigger than it really is. If you have a song that's recorded with a band, you think, if I just strum along it will sound small, but if I can play something of the bass line or something of the lead guitar and still keep the whole thing rolling, then that will sound more interesting. It'll be more of a complete thing. So really I'm trying to make more complete and bigger arrangements. I think a lot of acoustic players do.

The whole idea of open tunings comes from trying to make a bigger sound on the guitar, to try to make a guitar sing, to develop a singing line. An instrument like the guitar isn't a horn. It's similar to a piano. With a piano you have to work to make the line flow. With the guitar you have to work to make the line flow and use open tunings as a way of creating notes that hang over and ring. So you have drones and seconds, and fourths and fifths and sevenths—stuff that just hangs over to fill the sound out and sustain the sound and give it a fluidity, which is kind of a direction the acoustic guitar has taken over the last 30, 40, 50 years.

Ornamentation has always been a big thing for you. You'll sometimes play figures on one string with a lot of ornamentation, so that the notes almost seem to overlap, like on a bagpipe, which can only play one note at a time.

THOMPSON I'm very influenced by bagpipe music and fiddle music. It's a singing thing. It's trying to create a voice on an instrument. And a bagpipe is an instrument that tries to imitate a human voice.

It's imitating Gaelic singing.

THOMPSON Yeah, and so is a fiddle trying to imitate a human voice. So you try to make an instrument sing. When you bring an instrument into a tradition from the outside, you have to borrow things from existing tradition. So you borrow sounds and phrases. You try to make a guitar sound like a fiddle. Listening to D'Gary from Madagascar, it seems that his guitar sounds like a valiha, a Malagasy harp. So you just have to bend instruments to make them sound real and compatible.

Paul Simon

rom the '60s triumphs of Simon and Garfunkel to a long, extraordinarily diverse solo career, Paul Simon has left his mark on four decades of American music. In this exchange with Jeffrey Pepper Rodgers, Simon offers insights into how he makes use of music theory in his songwriting and delicate guitar work.

How conscious are you of the theory behind what you're playing? Are you working out the chords primarily by sound?

SIMON Yeah, of course, by sound, by what sounds the most interesting. But I can think of several possibilities of how to approach it, and then it's, which do you like best? Or, do you want to combine them in some different way? But always by ear.

When I'm standing up in front of an audience, I'm simplifying. I don't want to take too much of my attention to the guitar. I just want the guitar to be constant—nothing to worry about. I concentrate on blending with Artie [Garfunkel] and giving him a very secure, safe guitar part. If I make a mistake, he's the one who is stuck out there.

Guitar has been the basis of a lot of your music, but you've also transcended it in many ways, both through keyboard-based harmonies, as in Still Crazy After All These Years, *and through drum-based albums like* Rhythm of the Saints. *Have you done that to get past certain limitations of the guitar as a songwriting instrument, or to get away from certain progressions that the guitar might lead you toward?*

SIMON I take a much more pianistic approach to the writing, with leading tones and [paying attention to] what the bass is. . . .

It's not always the root in the bass. The bass line moves with a certain logic that dictates how the chords are voiced, as opposed to barre here, barre here, strum there. So for ballads, you can write more interesting changes with that approach on guitar.

That's something that I started to do quite a lot in the '70s, when I was studying with Chuck Israels, who is a bass player and composer, so the harmonic approach wasn't a guitaristic approach—it was with a bass player's and a composer's thinking. And really not that different than the way Howard [Morgen, Simon's guitar teacher] thinks as well. And then, of course, the African way is another style. Different styles become available to you if you live through them and play them. You can use the elements and find a way of expressing what you want to express, and have it shift from one style to another, and blend the styles. And that blending becomes your voice, your style of playing.

Do you think that learning a lot of chord theory and the like can be a trap, in that if you're aware of all these possibilities, you might feel you have to use them?

SIMON No, I don't think it's a trap. Simple is always a choice.

But some people seem to forget that choice.

SIMON Well, it's not the knowledge that's the trap. How you hear music, what your instinct is, is going to be how you express music. There may be a time when you want to express something that's more complex, and it would be nice to have that available to you if that were the case. And there are times when just the simplest of chords is going to be the most satisfying, and you would want to know when that moment had arrived.

So I don't think that knowledge is a trap at all; I think the more technique you have, the more options you have of expressing yourself. How you express yourself is your nature; it may be very moving, it may be artistic, and it may be banal, but it's not because you had too much knowledge.

Indigo Girls

Emily Saliers (left) and Amy Ray.

Since their debut in 1989, the Indigo Girls have riveted audiences with the interplay between Amy Ray's primal rock 'n' roll and Emily Saliers' softer, more reflective style. Both are versatile songwriters and guitarists who have branched out more and more into other stringed instruments (banjo, bouzouki, mandolin, baritone guitar . . .). In an interview with Jeffrey Pepper Rodgers, they explained how the different instruments affect the writing process and how they share their creations.

Did you start using all these new stringed instruments as a result of experimenting in your writing or because you were to trying broaden your sound on record?

SALIERS It was actually both. For instance, "Get Out the Map" is a song that I play banjo on, and I wrote it on banjo. But Amy wrote "Shame on You," and I played banjo on parts of it just for a different color. I wrote "Caramia" on electric guitar. It's the first song I've written on electric guitar. And then other instruments got added to other songs. Bouzouki got added for texture.

RAY Baritone guitar. Baritone guitar is something I've always loved. We just never had one, but Emily gave me one.

SALIERS We're both trying to grow.

Do you find that a new instrument leads you into different songwriting territory than you would get to otherwise?

SALIERS I think so. Although today we did a radio interview, and we were playing the song "Get Out the Map," which I wrote on banjo. I played it on guitar because I didn't have a banjo in the studio, and I realized that the chords are just like "Closer to Fine," so I guess that kind of blows that theory. I thought I'd written something different from that.

RAY Yeah, but what you did is write "Get Out the Map," whereas if you'd written it on guitar, you would have gone, 'This sounds like "Closer to Fine,"' and you would have never written the song.

How do you share new songs with each other?

SALIERS Sometimes we'll start songs or be playing them in sound check to test things, just for fun. So I'll start to hear snippets of Amy's ideas early on. By the time she finishes the songs, they'll be somewhat familiar to me. Last time around, I wrote my songs in a pretty short period of time and ended up playing a couple of them for her that I guess she'd never heard even parts of. And it's a loaded moment, you know. You want your partner to like your stuff.

RAY I sang a lot of my new songs in public before I actually played them for her. We had a long time off and we were very separate, and I was doing separate gigs, writers' nights, just to work in new material and figure out if I liked the songs I was writing. Maybe Emily heard something after I'd already played it for an audience, or maybe she was even in the audience and heard it the first time. So that kind of dilutes the loadedness of it a little bit.

Do you ever nix each other's songs or send each other back to the drawing board?

SALIERS No. Not typically at all. Sometimes we'll decide a song is better off if it's a solo song.

RAY Or make suggestions. We'll ask, "What do you think of this?" and the other person might say, "I think the chorus is too long" or "I think we should add a bridge" or "I'm missing this element." If the song's important enough for the person to have written it and believe in it themselves, then you've got to give it a chance.

SALIERS You have to have faith that the process is working, and you have to get used to someone else's ideas being added to your song. You're used to just singing the song alone, and you know it in an intimate and personal way, and then all of a sudden it's become something else. But for the most part, I have faith in the process of what Amy and I have done for so long, and while sometimes it's an adjustment at first, in the end it usually comes out being better.

RAY When I play alone, I tend to be very unstructured. I usually don't have a real definitive tempo. I start and stop and slow down and do things on any given night differently from the night before in the same song. When you play with somebody else, you can't really do that as much. So for me, the songs take on structure, which is good sometimes. But sometimes it's really hard for me to get used to.

Do you record yourself while you're writing?

RAY I do. I tape all the time I'm writing. [*To Emily*] Do you?

SALIERS No. Unless there's a certain thing I want to remember, like a guitar chord progression or a melody line. Then I'll tape it. But usually I'll just write down the notes.

RAY I never listen to tapes when they're done. Ever. I don't know why, but I always tape, 'cause it somehow makes me remember it better.

SALIERS Do you keep them?

RAY Yeah. It's a weird process. I never listen to them.

Both of your guitar styles have evolved quite a bit over the last ten years. How do you think your playing has developed?

RAY Obviously, we use a lot more tunings than we used to. I think all we used when we started was open D. And then Emily would use some Joni Mitchell–type tunings.

SALIERS Mary Chapin Carpenter taught me a couple of tunings, but I didn't start using them until "Galileo"—*Rites of Passage* [the tuning is D A D G B C, the same as for Carpenter's "The Moon and St. Christopher"].

RAY And I just turned to tunings as an alternative, you know, to have fun with it. "Center Stage" [from *Indigo Girls*] was in open D. I remember hearing the B-52s, that guy Ricky [Wilson]—he played every song they had in a different tuning. He never played anything in standard tuning, and I just remember thinking about that—it was really inspiring. The guitar became an endless spectrum at that point. I'm not a really good guitar player, so to change tunings opens up new worlds for me.

SALIERS We try to make it as expansive as we possibly can with just the two of us, not just for the sake of being expansive, but because it's more gratifying than, "Let's just play the same chords." Personally, I used to play much more jazz-oriented chords and was really influenced by this local singer-songwriter. And then I found after a while emotionally I just couldn't get as much out of playing that way. In some ways it's a lot easier technically to play in a more aggressive style, and emotionally it's much more accessible.

Jules Shear

Jules Shear is one of our most engaging songwriters ("If She Knew What She Wants" for the Bangles, "All through the Night" for Cyndi Lauper) as well as a highly respected solo artist whose albums include *Between Us* (High Street/Windham Hill), a song cycle of duets with Carole King, Curtis Stigers, Paula Cole, Rosanne Cash, and others. Behind Shear's songs lie highly unorthodox guitar and writing techniques, as he describes in this profile by Paul Zollo.

Jules Shear's songwriting is strongly affected by the idiosyncratic guitar technique he discovered at the age of 13. A lefty, he borrowed his brother Robby's Kay guitar, turned it upside-down, and tuned it to "what sounded like a chord." In fact, it was an open-G tuning, which he uses to this day (from low to high: E G B D G B), forming chords by pressing his right thumb down across all the strings. After months of playing only major chords on the guitar, he surmised that by leaving the lowest string tuned to E, he could create minor chords by including this note, and muffle it for majors. At first Shear was embarrassed by what he felt to be an aberrant approach to the guitar, but by the time he started appearing in coffeehouses at the age of 18, he said, "It was too late to go back."

Despite this admittedly primitive technique, or maybe because of it, the songs Shear concocts on the guitar are anything but primitive. Epitomizing Krishnamurti's famous quote, "Limitation creates form," Shear's music is both sophisticated and visceral, often achieving what he calls a melodic "ache"—that musical yearning that comes only from the perfect blend of chords and melody and words. It's a style that springs directly from the way he plays and views the guitar.

"There's nothing wrong with limitations," he said. "I know I write the songs I write because I look at the guitar in a different way than most people do. When I look down at the chords and the way I relate to what the chord is, it's like a different language than what other people are speaking. I think if you're just stuck as I am with these basic chords—all the major chords and all the minor chords—then you rely on the relationship between the melody and the chords. And I think that is one of the strongest things I do."

Shear is wise to the notion that pretty chords do not a pretty melody make. "I know writers who can play beautiful chords, and they rely on the beauty of the chord to write songs, and the songs don't turn out so well," he said. "It's much better to have a simple progression of chords with maybe one interesting, surprising chord in there, because then it really becomes juicy at that point. It becomes something that has an effect rather than a complete bombast, like putting someone in a space where everything is weird. But if you set it up that everything is fine and *then* something weird happens, it has a completely different effect."

Shear's songwriting process, like his guitar playing, is distinctively compelling. It starts with lyrics: "Some days I write just words. Just musings. Not a story, but maybe something a story could come from. Not a title, though sometimes titles come from that, too. It's really just thinking about life, the world, things that are happening. And then it's just a matter of phrasing it in a way that seems songlike. Not thinking about music or rhyming or if it's a bridge or a verse or a chorus. Just writing words."

The next morning Shear takes out his guitar and looks over these musings for the kernel of a song. "I go to my desk and look at my first page and say, 'What kind of song does this suggest to me?' Music usually comes pretty quickly, which makes me think there are a lot of musical ideas in the universe. If I'm in that space of wanting to fulfill a longing, I can usually do it in a short period of time. It's just a feeling that I want to get, and then it's a matter of matching up a melody and a chord change with the feeling that I want to get. I'm not relying on anything that I've done before. And I don't know how to do it. It's completely instinctual. I'm just longing to hear something, and I try to satisfy that. Basically, I'm just groping."

As opposed to Bob Dylan, who said that the hardest thing to do in songwriting is to reconnect with an idea after you've stopped working on it, Shear forces himself to stop. After a full morning of songwriting, he breaks until the late evening, when he can return to the song with some semblance of clarity and objectivity. Around midnight he listens to the tape of that morning's work. But to ensure that he hears it with fresh ears, he plays it back at a faster speed than that at which it was recorded.

"This way it sounds like somebody else's song altogether," he said. "And then I can judge it. This way I don't get distracted by the sound of my own singing or performance. And everything is compressed, so I don't have time to think about what is coming next; I can just experience it. I'm able to react to it as a piece of music and not just as something I wrote. I know this sounds like an unusual method, but it's really helpful to me. Things will *really* become clear to me at that point. And it's a big event for me, because I'm going to discover what I did that day. And sometimes the news is good and sometimes the news is bad, but at least I get news, rather than just working in a vacuum."

Even if the news he receives is less than cheerful, Shear never abandons the song. "I'm a finisher," he said. "I like to get songs done. Most songwriters are notoriously lazy, and they use any excuse to not finish a song. It *is* easier to go out to dinner. But sometimes you do finish a song that seemed to be going nowhere, and it comes out great. Or even if it doesn't, the next time you write a song you will write something as a reaction to what you wrote before. And you might write something that's amazing, something you wouldn't have written had you not written the one that wasn't good. I think finishing all songs is important for that reason."

Gillian Welch and David Rawlings

With just two starkly beautiful albums, *Revival* and *Hell among the Yearlings,* Gillian Welch and David Rawlings established themselves as one of the most powerful new songwriting voices of the '90s. In a conversation with Simone Solondz, the Nashville-based duo explained how they compose and arrange together.

"Dave is really good with plot development and is a really good editor," said Welch. "After I get as far as I can with the initial inspiration—spitting out as much as I possibly can—then we start working on it together. The grueling part is filling in the gaps. Most of my job as a writer happens after the initial inspiration. I need to turn on my brain and come up with words that match the illogical [intuitive] stuff. The whole process is about being as transparent as you can be. I never want anyone to think, 'Ooh-hoo, that was really clever. That's good writing.'

"Other genres might be more cerebral, and people might appreciate clever wordplay or a rhyme. But in the more traditional genre we work in, I think it's a mistake if anyone's aware of me as a writer. I just want them to hear the story and the character and the emotion. The aesthetic of transparency is what we deal with all the time."

Both partners insist that they're not trying to sound old-fashioned or "timeless." "Hopefully, the stuff sounds contemporary," Welch said, "because that's what it is. These stories have never been told before, and these words have never been strung together before. The transparent part is that I hope people have an emotional response to it."

But the duo's influences, especially Welch's, are primarily the old-time, gospel, and country artists of the '20s and '30s. "I had a music teacher very early on in grade school [in Los Angeles] who taught us Carter Family and Woody Guthrie songs, like 'Does Your Horse Carry Double?'" Welch recalled. "I started playing guitar when I was eight, and the first songs I played were traditional songs, folk songs. When I went away to college at [the University of California] Santa Cruz, I got into the bluegrass community and I started hearing all those original recordings for the first time. It had a very, very strong impact on me, particularly the Stanley Brothers. When I heard the Stanley Brothers, I pretty much knew what I wanted to do for the rest of my life."

Welch doesn't really maintain a strict writing schedule but tries to get something down every day. Her approach may be somewhat atypical in that she doesn't write a lot of songs and then choose the best ones for public dissemination. "I think some people finish everything and then look at what they've got and pick the songs that are stand-outs," she said. "With us, the songs don't get completely done if we don't like them. I pursue 90 percent of the ideas that I have. I don't know what percentage of those become finished songs. Sometimes I consider tunes fatally flawed, and I just drop them. But if I think it's a good idea, I'll do anything. Two years on the drawing board is fine."

"A lot of times, the idea is so small," Rawlings added. "She'll have a really great verse, but we'll bang our heads against the wall for a while and nothing will follow it up. Sometimes what we find is that the first two lines of the [original] four-line verse are the first two lines of the song, and the last two are the last two lines of the song. And then you've got to stretch it and fill in the middle." This is the process that helped them finish the song "Barroom Girls," recorded on *Revival*. Most of the song is description and commentary; the only action that takes place is a girl getting up out of bed. The original verse Welch came up with, which was later used to frame the entire song, was this:

Oh the night came undone like a party dress
And fell at her feet in a beautiful mess
Last night's spangles and yesterday's pearls
Are the bright morning stars of the barroom girls

The addition of the banjo deeply affected the songs written for the duo's second album, *Hell among the Yearlings*. Welch believes that the banjo adds a nice texture but provides its own set of challenges. "The banjo songs tend to be more repetitive," she said, "because the rhythm is so incessant and also because I'm not really worrying about chord changes as much. It's more modal, and I use the drone string a lot. I just play the melody and that's it. It's a little bit hypnotic."

Rawlings pointed out that all of the songs Welch wrote on banjo encompass a series of melodically identical verses rather than the verse-chord-bridge structure modern listeners have become accustomed to. "Almost every song on *Revival* has a chorus, and almost no songs on [*Hell among the Yearlings*] do," he said.

This change in basic structure was entirely unintentional. "I had no control over it," Welch said. "I think that your brain just works that way. You get a template stuck in your head. I used to be a photographer, and a teacher of mine told me not to take too many pictures without printing them, because you will keep taking the same damn picture. If you look at it, you'll be formatting it exactly the same—you'll have a horizontal in the same place and a vertical in the same place, and it'll be basically the same contrast. And I think it happens with songs too. If you don't step away from them enough, you'll just keep writing the same song."

David Crosby

Along with his friend and sometimes collaborator Joni Mitchell, David Crosby helped to pioneer the use of alternate guitar tunings in pop music, and he continues to use them to craft evocative songs for the reunited Crosby, Stills, Nash, and Young and for the band CPR, featuring his son James Raymond on keyboards and Jeff Pevar on lead guitar. Crosby described his songwriting explorations in this interview with Simone Solondz.

Do the words usually come to you first?

CROSBY It happens every which way, but yeah, very often. I had the set of changes for "Rusty and Blue" [*CPR*] for a couple of years before it [came together]. I'm not sure who writes the stuff.

It feels more like channeling?

CROSBY Well, your head's got a lot of levels, right? The verbal crystallization level that I'm talking to you with right now isn't necessarily the one that does the writing. There's maybe a level that makes longer leaps, and that one gets a shot at inputting very often with me just as I'm going to sleep. The busy mind kind of cacks out, and this level, where I think a lot of the writing goes on, gets a shot at the controls.

And you wake up and write it all down?

CROSBY Yeah. One of the big effects on my writing was [Joni] Mitchell telling me to write stuff down. She said, "David, you throw away more good phrases in an afternoon than most people can come up with in a week. What's wrong with you, you brainless twit? Write your shit down!" And I learned from her that if you get even two words in a row that mean something, that make you feel something, you should write them down. So I do.

I can think of one song that was two complete different sets of words written years apart that I showed to a friend of mine who I wrote many songs with—Craig Doerge—and he said, "These sort of relate. Did you notice that?" No. Are you out of your tree? He said,

"Yeah they do," and we wound up with "Night Time for the Generals" [on the live *King Biscuit Flower Hour*].

How does the guitar affect your writing process? If you're working in open tunings, are you hearing chords that you can't play in standard?

CROSBY That's the reason for going into open tunings in the first place. I would listen to [John] Coltrane, and here's this guy who wouldn't stick to a normal mode, so [pianist] McCoy Tyner would have to invent very dense, broad kinds of tone clusters, and they would be beautiful. And I would want to play that, and I couldn't. I'm not a great player. I'm not gifted. But in a nonstandard tuning I can.

So it starts with hearing a chord. Do you then go to the piano to work out the notes in the chord?

CROSBY No, I'm not schooled. I can't do that. I can't tell you the names of any of the chords I play.

So how do you figure out how to tune the strings?

CROSBY That happens sometimes by experimenting. I found the tuning for "Rusty in Blue" and "Tracks in the Dust" and a couple of other songs in C G D D A D by experimenting, by goofing around. Other times it's a friend. The tuning for "Climber," D A D G C D, came when a guy who plays guitar here in the [Santa Barbara] area, Mark Owen, was playing something. And I immediately found a bunch of stuff he hadn't found. The next time I showed him one of mine, he found five things in it that I never found, and I'd been playing in it for years.

He found chords?

CROSBY Yes. And that's the process. None of us owns any of it, right? I mean every series of notes, the most complex ideas that the most complex musicians in the world have played, some guy sitting around with a flute in the Nile delta played two million years before him [*laughter*]. It's called the folk process. You just naturally pass music along.

With a guitar, you take a regular tuning [*strums a standard-tuned guitar*] and the first thing you do is tune that low E down to a D because then it makes your D chord [*strums*] sound like that. And you go, "Ooh! That's cool! I really like that!" And you're hooked. From that day on, you're a lost soul.

Joni Mitchell

One of our most original and influential songwriters, Joni Mitchell has found an endless stream of harmonic ideas in a guitar style based on ever-changing tunings (50-plus and counting) and a painterly right-hand touch. In this profile by Jeffrey Pepper Rodgers, she illuminates the guitar techniques and inspirations behind her songs.

How does Mitchell discover the tunings and fingerings that create her expansive harmonies and what she calls "modern chords"? Here's how she describes the process: "You're twiddling and you find the tuning. Now the left hand has to learn where the chords are, because it's a whole new ballpark, right? So you're groping around, looking for where the chords are, using very simple shapes. Put it in a tuning and you've got four chords immediately—open, barre five, barre seven, and your higher octave, like half fingering on the 12th. Then you've got to find where your minors are and where the interesting colors are—that's the exciting part.

"Sometimes I'll tune to some piece of music and find [an open tuning] that way, sometimes I just find one going from one to another, and sometimes I'll tune to the environment. Like 'The Magdalene Laundries' [from *Turbulent Indigo;* the tuning is B F♯ B E A E]: I tuned to the day in a certain place, taking the pitch of bird songs and the general frequency sitting on a rock in that landscape."

Mitchell likens her use of continually changing tunings to sitting down at a typewriter on which the letters are rearranged each day. It's inevitable that you get lost and type some gibberish, and those mistakes are actually the main reason to use this system in the first place. "If you're only working off what you know, then you can't grow," she said. "It's only through error that discovery is made, and in order to discover you have to set up some sort of situation with a random element, a strange attractor, using contemporary physics terms. The more I can surprise myself, the more I'll stay in this business, and the twiddling of the notes is one way to keep the pilgrimage going. You're constantly pulling the rug out from under yourself, so you don't get a chance to settle into any kind of formula."

To date, Mitchell said that she has used 51 tunings. This number is so extraordinarily high in part because her tunings have lowered steadily over the years, so some tunings recur at several pitches. Generally speaking, her tunings started at a base of open E and dropped to D and then to C, and these days some even plummet to B or A in the bass. This evolution reflects the steady lowering of her voice since the '60s, a likely consequence of heavy smoking.

When Mitchell performs an older song today, she typically uses a lowered version of the original tuning. "Big Yellow Taxi," originally in open E (E B E G♯ B E), is now played in open C (C G C E G C, the same as open E dropped two whole steps). She recorded "Cherokee Louise" on *Night Ride Home* with the tuning D A E F♯ A D; when she performed it on the Canadian TV show *Much Music* in 1995, she played it in C G D E G C—a whole step lower. In some cases, the same relative tuning pops up in different registers for different songs: "Cool Water" (*Chalk Mark in a Rain Storm*) and "Slouching towards Bethlehem" (*Night Ride Home*) are in D A E G A D; a half step down, C♯ G♯ D♯ F♯ G♯ C♯, is the tuning for "My Secret Place" (*Chalk Mark*); another half step lower, C G D F G C, is the tuning for "Night Ride Home"; and a half step below that, B F♯ C♯ E F♯ B, is the tuning for "Hejira."

These connections allow Mitchell, in some cases, to carry fingerings from one tuning to another and find a measure of consistency, but each tuning has its own little universe of sounds and possibilities. "You never really can begin to learn the neck like a standard player, linearly and orderly," she said. "You have to think in a different way, in moving blocks. Within the context of moving blocks, there are certain things that you'll try from tuning to tuning that will apply."

Mitchell has come up with a way to categorize her tunings into families, based on the number of half steps between the notes of adjacent strings. "Standard tuning's numerical system is 5 5 5 4 5, with the knowledge that your bass string is E, right?" she said. "Most of my tunings at this point are 7 5 or 7 7, where the 5 5 usually is on the bottom. The 7 7 and the 7 5 family tunings are where I started from." Examples of 7 5 tunings are D A D G B D (used for "Free Man in Paris," *Court and Spark*) and C G C E G C ("Amelia," *Hejira*): in both cases, the fifth string is tuned to the *seventh* fret of the sixth string, and the fourth string is tuned to the *fifth* fret of the fifth string. Similarly, examples of 7 7 tunings are C G D G B D ("Cold Blue Steel and Sweet Fire," *For the Roses*) and C♯ G♯ D♯ E♯ G♯ C♯ ("Sunny Sunday," *Turbulent Indigo*): the intervals between the sixth and fifth strings, and the fifth and fourth strings, are seven frets.

Mitchell continued, "However, the dreaded 7 9 family—I have about seven songs in 7 9 tunings—are in total conflict with the 7 5 and the 7 7 families. They're just outlaws. They're guaranteed bass clams [*laughs*], 'cause the thumb gets used to going automatically into these shapes, and it has to make this slight adaptation." Mitchell's 7 9 songs include "Borderline," "Turbulent Indigo," and "How Do You Stop" (*Turbulent Indigo*), all of which are in the tuning B F♯ D♯ D♯ F♯ B.

Just to confuse the fingers further, Mitchell also has some renegade tunings in which she's written only one song. Consider the tuning for "Black Crow," from *Hejira:* B♭ B♭ D♭ F A♭ B♭, with the fifth and sixth strings an octave apart. By Mitchell's numerical system, this would be a 12 3 tuning—a very long way from 7 7 or 7 5, and a thousand miles from standard tuning.

David Wilcox

Perhaps the best known of the brilliant crop of singer-songwriters who emerged in the late '80s, David Wilcox uses byzantine combinations of alternate tunings and partial capos (which press down only certain strings and leave others open) to inspire new ideas. In this conversation with James Jensen, Wilcox describes how he lets the guitar take the lead in the song-writing process.

Do you play enough in each of the tunings you utilize to become fluent in them?

WILCOX I hope not. What I aim for is to always have that beginner's mind-set, to always be starting. The thing that the guitar gave me was a sense that I wasn't just playing it, I was listening to it, and it was playing things I couldn't play. I love that feeling. I like to get lost and find a new way home, and that's why any time I start to know my way around a tuning, I change it. I used to think I couldn't write a song without a new tuning, and that's often the case, but I think there are more songs than tunings [*laughs*].

One thing I enjoy is playing in the key of G while the guitar is tuned to open C [from bottom to top, C G C G C E], or playing in the key of G while in D A D G A D tuning. Ry Cooder has been doing that for quite some time, but I didn't know, so when I learned "Tattler" off his *Paradise and Lunch* album I thought that his guitar was in a double dropped-D [D A D G B D]. Actually, it's in open G [D G D G B D], and it's so much easier in the right tuning, but I never thought that he'd be playing in a different key than that of the open tuning.

I think that there are some wonderful voicings you get when you play in an open tuning outside of its tonic center, and I really love using a major-key open tuning but playing it so that the song is in the key of the chord that's maybe on the second fret, so it comes out in sort of a modal, minor, fun thing.

How do you get ideas for the melody and lyrics?

WILCOX Songwriting for me is based mostly on my belief that the guitar knows the song. If I listen to the guitar, put it into some weird tuning, and begin to experiment, it plays me a melody. I say to the guitar, "Wow, that's beautiful, what's it about?" and the guitar replies, "How does it make you feel?" And I might say that it makes me think about this or that, and the guitar says, "Well, that's probably what it's about then."

At that point I ask, "What's next?" and the guitar usually responds by saying, "It depends on what the lyrics are about. Why don't you start writing, and I'll tell you the rest." So I start writing ideas and the guitar says, "Stop right there! This is the part— you've got to put these words with this phrase." And I say, " Oh guitar, you're killin' me!"

It's kind of like the monkeys and the typewriters thing, where if you have enough monkeys playing on enough typewriters one will eventually type out the sonnets of Shakespeare: that's my method of songwriting. If you're writing songs, you can have a lot of talent or a lot of time, and I choose the time method. I think that if you know what you like and have a way of creating interesting mistakes that will give you new variations—for me it's open tunings—then the laws of probability are in your favor. You will have an endless supply of new ideas, and if you continue to sort through and store them on a tape recorder, you can gather these great musical ideas as if you had the talent to make them up, when it was really the guitar that wrote all the songs.

When did you first get into modifying your own capos so that you could stop only certain strings and leave others open?

WILCOX That was around 1978 or '79. They didn't have Kyser capos then, but I did have a capo that I could cut the treble or bass side out of, and I really loved those kinds of open voicings.

Did you use these capos in conjunction with standard tuning?

WILCOX Mostly with open tunings.

Where did you get the idea to combine these partial capos with open tunings?

WILCOX Watching Richie Havens and the way he would fret those beautiful chords over the top of the neck and let the two unwound strings ring. I figured I could get a capo to do that, and I could play on top of it. The goal, for me, was to get piano chords—chords that have close clusters. I like having a nice roll in the middle of the chord to get sounds that you don't ordinarily hear on a guitar. With capos that are cut, you can have strings that are a half step apart right next to each other and get that nice little added ninth roll or suspended fourth. . . .

If I could contribute anything to guitar playing it would be this notion that it's not something you do to the guitar, it's something the guitar does to you. You need to listen to it and give it some leeway, let it play what it wants to play. Get your fingers off those strings and let them ring; don't always be trying to wrestle it to the ground.

I am so grateful for the enjoyment I've gotten out of the sound of the guitar. It really saved my life.

Writing Your First Song

Elizabeth Papapetrou

Writing a song is a gift to yourself—and sometimes a gift to the world. Song is one of the most powerful communication tools we have as human beings: a slice of life encapsulated in words, melody, and accompaniment. Many of us would like to write songs but find it hard to get started. We find it very intimidating to commit ourselves to words, notes, and chords and then to paper, recordings, and listeners' ears. Or, once we have started, we find it pretty much impossible to develop ideas into satisfactory songs. Here are some simple techniques that will help you get started and help you develop your ideas into songs that work.

MODIFYING AN EXISTING SONG

If getting the ball rolling is particularly intimidating, I encourage you to pick out a song that you admire and know the lyrics and melody to. It doesn't matter if you can't play the song. Remember that this is an exercise with the sole purpose of easing you slowly into your own creativity. The results will not be judged. Once you've chosen the song, choose a verse you like the feel of and rewrite it. One approach is to keep the same melody and write new words that fit the rhythm and the narrative purpose for that part of the song. You can also try leaving the words alone and rewriting the melody. This might be a little harder because the melodies of our favorite songs tend to get deeply entrenched in our memory. One way to help make this technique work is to change the key of the song. A third approach is to create a new chord structure that fits with the original lyrics and melody. This can be a lot of fun for more experienced players who understand chord progressions, inversions, and modes, but it might be intimidating to the less experienced musician. If you ever do feel intimidated during these exercises, try taking a small step— just changing one line or even one or two words, for example—rather than a huge stride.

FINDING INSPIRATION

OK, so you're ready to go solo. What are you going to write about? The single most common inspiration for songs is love: the lack of it, the hope for it, the experience of it, the loss of it. You might not want to bare your soul so intimately in your first song, though, so let's look at some other options.

Experiences. Has anything notable happened to you lately? Some happenstance that changed your way of seeing life, yourself, someone else, the world? Did you witness something unusual? Remember a childhood memory, perhaps? There's lots of potential here.

Political causes. Do you feel strongly about a particular cause? Write a song about it. This is a deep well of inspiration for the folk movement.

History. Another great source for folkies. Lots of rich material.

People. Think about someone you admire, someone who inspires you.

Objects. This may sound like an odd suggestion, but objects have inspired many great songs. Artists write songs about bridges, buildings, ships . . . day-old banana pudding.

Fantasies and made-up occurrences. They can be impossible, fanciful, or just plain untrue. One of my favorite songs, "Something About Him" by Brady Earnhart, was written about a school days experience the writer invented.

Dreams. I was going to put this under fantasies, but there are invented situations that can and do come true.

Whatever subject you choose, you need to look carefully at how you think and feel about it. This is what actors mean when they ask, "What's my motivation?" Does the subject make you feel anger, pain, joy, tenderness? Where do your thoughts take you concerning this subject? At this point it would be a good idea to take notes on your thoughts and feelings. They'll help you build a framework for the song and give shape to the way your words and melody develop.

SONG STRUCTURE

Writing a song is almost always an exercise that involves alternating structured thought with unstructured: intermittently letting go of intellectual control and expectations and allowing your creativity to flow. Structured thought allows order to be maintained, and unstructured brings in the unexpected or unconscious.

At this point, you need to decide what kind of song structure you're going to use. Do you want to use a structure you're familiar with from another artist's work? Or do you want to let your poetic and melodic muse run free and just see what structure comes out? If there's any doubt concerning structure, I'd recommend starting with a simple 12-bar blues. This structure has been hardwired into the musical awareness of the Western world for the last half century. It's also sparse, so it encourages minimal use of words and limited melodic movement. Repetition is fundamental to the form.

In a 12-bar blues, the first line (sung over the first four bars) usually introduces the core subject matter and then comments on it, often in a way that brings tension to the subject. Most of the third bar and all of the fourth bar are generally instrumental. The next four bars might repeat the subject and expand on the comments and tension, and the last word usually rhymes with the last word of the first line. The seventh and eighth bars are usually instrumental. The last line should bring some kind of resolution to the subject, much as the melody and chordal turnaround brings resolution to the music. The 12th bar is most often the turnaround—a chordal/melodic progression, usually without words, that brings the song back to the top, to the next verse, which is structured like the first.

LYRICS

For most songwriters, the words of a song come first. Others start with the melody or with a chord progression and add the other elements one at a time. And for some, lyrics and melody come at the same time. Let's start with the lyrics.

Go back to your notes on the general subject matter of the song you want to write. Do any of the words and phrases jump out at you? Do some of them seem to fit together either because of their meaning or because of their sound or rhythm?

For our 12-bar blues, I wrote down a few words about being a new songwriter, what it might mean and what it might feel like: *trying to write a song I love songs want to do it music in my soul scary new going to do it determined.* Looking at these words, I came up with the line:

I'm tryin' to write a song and it's kinda new to me

OK, that works. Note that I picked an easy rhyme ("me") and remembered that this has to fit over three or so bars of a midpaced blues. For the second line, I wanted to repeat the core subject and comment further. I looked at the word *scary* and got:

I'm tryin' to write a song and I'm scared as I can be

In order to stick to the standard 12-bar blues arrangement (which is now playing in my head), we need to add a brief pause to the lyrics after the word *it's* in the first line and *I'm* in the second. This leaves us with:

> *I'm tryin' to write a song and it's . . . kinda new to me*
> *I'm tryin' to write a song and I'm . . . scared as I can be*

Hmm. That's fine. Now I need a resolution. Going back to my original notes, I find the obvious resolution of "going to do it." An alliteration—several words in a row starting with the same consonant—jumps out at me:

> *But I'm gonna get it goin'*

I've got to admit that I'm a sucker for nice alliterations, and this one is particularly appealing because *gonna get it goin'* comes with a built-in rhythm. Another look at my notes does nothing for me, so I write down the first thing that comes into my head:

> *But I'm gonna get it goin' . . . and I'm almost there you see*

Now, I quite like the *almost,* but the *there you see* is pretty lame. Still, I never intended to leave things like that. I just wrote this line to help me come up with something more appropriate. Next I decide to be positive and note that I've come to this point fairly easily—almost painlessly—and get excited about:

> *But I'm gonna get it goin' almost painlessly*

A few minutes' detachment gets me to see that it's an untidy rhyme and that *painlessly* somehow doesn't fit with *gonna get it goin'.* So I fiddle with *painlessly* and find *pain-free,* which I like the feel of. When I attach it to the line, I get:

> *But I'm gonna get it goin' . . . and I'm almost there pain-free*

So, now we have:

> *I'm tryin' to write a song and it's . . . kinda new to me*
> *I'm tryin' to write a song and I'm . . . scared as I can be*
> *But I'm gonna get it goin'   and I'm almost there pain-free*

A brief go at singing this verse shows me that *tryin'* falls on the 1 of the first and fifth bars and that the pause in each line falls on the 1, with the next word starting on the off-beat. I'm fairly certain that the blues arrangement in my head will work best for this song, but I'll try a few different feels and even recite the words aloud a few times (as straight as I can) to see if any other feel comes up. No, the blues feel seems to work best, but one thing that did jump out at me is that *gonna get it goin'* begs to have the pace of the rhythm accelerated for those words.

Now I'll sing the verse aloud unaccompanied until I'm happy with the way it flows. Only after this step do I pick up my guitar. It turns out I'm singing in the key of E minor, which leads me to a standard blues chord progression with Em, A7, and B7.

Alright! Our song is begun. I say *our* because I encourage you to write further verses based on the same structure. Perhaps when you're done with this song, you'll write your own from scratch. Remember to follow the steps we've discussed and not to bite off more than you can chew at any given moment. Good luck!

Luring the Muse

Patty Larkin

It's all about inspiration. For Hemingway it was Paris, women, hunting, booze, Idaho, women, Africa, booze, hunting—not necessarily in that order. But how do you write a song? Gaining access to the muse is the main thing. Sometimes a song falls into your lap. This is a gift. Other times a song is the result of craft and work and sweat. Still other times, during a dry spell, you can't believe you ever wrote a song, and you would do anything to write again. The desire becomes a dull ache in the back of your psyche, from which you seek relief in any form: a new guitar, a loud amplifier, late nights, early mornings, lots of coffee, travel, meditation, wine, Oprah, sensory deprivation.

You are not alone. I have found no guaranteed access to the muse, but I have learned how to open the door a crack for a peek inside, a glimpse that sometimes leads to insight, that sometimes leads to inspiration, that sometimes leads to a new song. What follows is a foray into that search for the muse.

WRITING FROM BOTH SIDES OF THE BRAIN

The important thing is to write. It took me years to realize that songs don't happen unless I write them. Sounds simple. I think of it like fishing—you can't catch anything unless you go to the water's edge and put the line in. So I set myself up to catch whatever falls into my lap. When I am starting a writing cycle—because it goes in cycles for me—I begin with my journal. For 15 minutes before I play my guitar, I write down whatever comes into my head. It's drivel for the most part, but it's *my* drivel. I get used to putting words to my feelings. After a while themes show themselves. After another while I attempt a poem of free verse, a stream of consciousness that forces me to be more specific. I begin to use images and metaphors—you know, the stuff you learned in English class.

I don't judge my journal. I don't think I have ever pulled a line from it. It helps me begin to focus on something other than the mundane. I start to read books that appeal to me. Sometimes I read aloud. I want to know that words have worked for somebody else. Sometimes I read books on writing. They give me hope. If at any time I think of a phrase or a line I like, I write it in the back of my songwriting notebook. I start to listen harder. Lines like "He was much too good-looking for his height" ("Johnny Was a Pyro") and "The Book I'm Not Reading" came out of real-life conversations. What you hear around you becomes fuel for the fire. I listen to music. I listen to music I would never play—Beck and Counting Crows. I listen to Dylan and Leonard Cohen and Mary Margaret O'Hara, to angry young women and famous old men. I want to create a hunger to write. I want to witness beauty in order to create it. I want to feel passionate about what I do.

WHILE YOUR GUITAR GENTLY SPEAKS

I am a guitar-focused songwriter, which means that my melodies and harmonic sense are derived from the resonant instrument perched on my lap. The guitar intrigues me and makes me want to vocalize. The guitar creates an atmosphere—the sounds and textures that become songs. Sometimes I hear what I want to write before I sit down with the guitar. I visualize it on the guitar, not in any special way, just simply. Before I wrote "You and Me," I was overcome with the desire to play a big fat open A chord. With "Booth of Glass" I knew I wanted to capo up the neck and fingerpick something pretty. I'll experiment with guitar sounds and techniques, and the licks I like can spawn new songs. On the other hand, I find that when I write story songs I want simple chords—open G, D, or C. I just need to get the voice of the narrator out.

Very subtle changes in the chords can help guide the melody for me. In "I Told Him That My Dog Wouldn't Run" (aka "Dog"), I was writing in my journal and I picked up the guitar and played an open C, then an F with a G in it (Fadd9). I played it in this form:

The added tension of the open G on the third string drew me in. The melody goes to the root of the chord, the F on the fourth string, and sits there at the end of each phrase. The result is a dissonance that creates a feeling of uneasiness, a lack of resolution. It's unsettling, and it fit perfectly with the lyric. In "Johnny Was a Pyro" the chorus goes, "What am I doing with this ring on my hand?" I am playing an Asus4 chord and singing the resolution before I go to the A chord. More tension. I search out these curious spots in other writers' work—and I look for it in my own writing. I want to go outside the lines. By holding the melody note too long or by adding tension to the chord, I can draw the listener in, emphasize the lyric, and create atmosphere.

THE ALTERNATIVES

Another way to add color to a harmonic progression is through the use of alternate tunings. If you play piano, you know that you can get plenty of dissonance by playing the middle C and the D next to it at the same time (as in "Chopsticks"). As guitarists we are a bit more challenged to play those two notes at the same time on the fretboard. With open or alternate tunings these sounds become easily available. In my song "Carolina" (in C G C G C D tuning), one of my favorite chords is an Am11. The top three strings ring out—B, C, D—going right up the minor scale, so you get this beautiful little run on the treble strings:

If you take your index finger off the fifth string, the chord progression descends while the top three strings are suspended above it. Somewhere in the back of my mind I know I am going from the IV minor to the V chord, but I don't care. I just like it.

When I go to alternate tunings it's because I am looking for inspiration. I can get drone strings, ringing notes, and languid tensions that are not available to me in standard. I want to be surprised by what I play. I don't want to think too much. To that end, I seldom analyze what I play in alternate tunings. There are some tunings I am very familiar with— D A D G A D, dropped D, open C with a D on top (C G C G C D)—and they still fascinate me. If I'm feeling the pressure of a great void, I turn to technique books and publications in order to bend my mind with new tunings. I'll tailor a tuning to fit my needs. When I rearranged Laura Nyro's "Poverty Train," I remembered reading an interview with Emmylou Harris in *Acoustic Guitar* where she described a low tuning: A A C♯ E A C♯. I thought that it would work well on a low, gnarly guitar part. It gave me the courage to try something different. I ended up with A A A E A B and used a variation of that tuning for "Anyway the Main Thing Is" (A A A E A A) on my new album *Regrooving the Dream*

(Vanguard). Ignorance is bliss. When I wrote "Tango," I thought the guitar was in standard tuning, and I picked it up and played an open D. It was in D A D G A D, so I let go of the high E string and voilà, a song fell out. The world of alternate tunings is a land of no rules. You are likely to enter the maze dazed and confused and exit it in a creative state of grace.

I am looking for connections all the time. What note can I hang out to dry? What notes connect the next chord to this one? You can get these kinds of runs (B, C, D, open strings, etc.) in standard tuning (see *Fingerstyle Cross-Picking Solos,* Mel Bay), but there is something delicious about an open or alternate tuning. I checked out Richard Thompson's instructional cassettes on Homespun, and I have since written four songs in his F G D G C D tuning: "Monte Vista," "The Road," "Closest Thing," and "Rear View Mirror." The tonal center is on the fifth string, the open G. So when you go to the open F on the sixth string, the world turns and becomes very modal sounding. If you play all the strings starting at the fifth string, it sounds very ancient with a wealth of melody notes. Descending the whole step to the sixth string while muting the fifth string sends you back half a millennium. It is this brave new world of discovery that leads me on. I find that a friend or an instructor can be helpful in revealing the sweet spots of a new tuning, and then I set out on my own from there.

THE JOY OF TECH

When I come up with anything of interest, I immediately put it on tape. I record it on a cheap little handheld tape recorder that sits nonjudgmentally and unobtrusively on my desk. I note any tuning information or personality quirks right on the tape, so that I don't return two months later and wonder what was going on.

I think it's important to keep the critic off your shoulder during the writing process. I just want to get it out, then analyze it and critique it later. Most of my songs initially appear as first verse and chorus. I may know what's worth keeping right from the start, but I want to keep that channel to the muse open—the beta state, the subconscious, the white light.

It's about thinking differently, connecting with something beyond yourself. If I get really stuck on a lyric, I ask myself, "What am I trying to say? Does it ring true?" Even if it's fiction, I want it to be honest. I want to tell the truth. I want the songs to capture the essence of my experience or the flavor of my observations. It's like centering a piece of clay on a potter's wheel. If it's not centered, the whole thing crumbles.

TRIAL BY FIRE: PLAYING OUT

I've just recently (in the last decade) gotten to the point where I can play partially written songs for other people, works in progress. The real test is to play the finished product out. It's why I am a performing songwriter. Performing the song reveals its foibles; the glue and the cracks show up in the light. It becomes painfully apparent that the song is only as strong as its weakest line.

You must be happy with the results of your work, because you will be singing this thing for the next several years. Does the song capture the feeling you originally intended? Is it done? It's up to you to decide. I've begun to relate to Leonard Cohen, who has said that some songs have taken him ten years to finish. Get it as airtight as you can, open the door, let it out, and have fun. That is, after all, why we do this in the first place.

Listening to Your Guitar

Don McLean

I n all my years as a songwriter, the guitar has been my main lifeline, the medium through which I receive musical ideas on my mental transmission line. It's a mysterious process—sometimes I feel like a Morse code operator taking down messages from an unknown source that only I can understand. That's as far as I'll go on that point since I'm Don, not Shirley, McLean.

To write with the guitar in this way, you have to really love the specific guitar you use. Gordon Stoker of the Jordanaires told me that when Elvis got his Martin D-28 with the leather cover, it was never out of his sight or out of his hands, and he loved it more than anything he ever owned. Think about Willie Nelson's old guitar. We all know how he feels about it, but the feelings he gets are his own, and surely they propel his need to sing and write. So you've got to have a real marriage with a particular guitar and forsake all others, except to pick now and then.

Your instrument has to look right when you wear it. When you strap it on it should give you the feeling of Superman when he emerges from a phone booth with his cape flowing. You want to have a sense of romance, like Roy Rogers feels when he's astride Trigger. This enhanced sense of self leads to the belief that you can now surprise yourself with what this new Superperson can create.

Having the right guitar, of course, just sets the stage for the hard part—practice. Any gunslinger worth his or her salt, besides looking cool, must be fast on the draw. In order to back up your new attitude and persona you must practice constantly so that everything you do on the guitar flows effortlessly.

SEARCHING FOR SONGS

I have many ways of writing songs, but here is my guitar way. First I try to hit on an idea that is pregnant with possibilities and has not been done before. In order to be sure of this, the songwriter must know thousands of songs from every musical area—jazz, pop standards, blues, early rock, some classical melodies, folk. . . . Second, I think of a title that is hard-hitting and poetic. Third, I sit with a guitar and a small tape recorder, several pencils, and lots of blank paper. Then I fiddle around with chords and funny little guitar figures while I sing a melody, riffing off the figures or chord changes. Soon a pattern emerges and a lyric form is established.

Then I stop. I look at this embryonic song idea and try to hear the form that is emerging. I put the guitar down and write more lyrics, expanding on the idea, using the form I've established by working off the guitar figures or chord changes. For example, play this progression from C to C augmented to F minor:

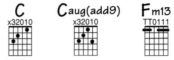

Do you see how this simple chord change can inspire you to write a melody? This pattern is the basis for Roy Orbison's song "Crying." In the case of my song "Wonderful Baby," I started playing a B♭ chord without the barre, and when I went down to the A, it was so pretty:

Then I went from the B♭ chord to this G form:

That G sounds so nice leading to a C, and when I put all these moves together, I wound up with this progression:

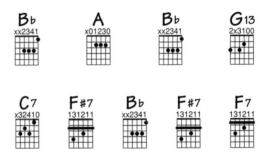

While I'm working on an idea like this, I'm recording everything. Then I listen back to this big mess and pick out the lyrics and musical elements that sound good. I do not read music, but I hear it. What I mean by that is, I hear the song in my head, and I'm just trying to figure out how to get it out of my guitar and into the tape recorder. I pay no attention to any commercial rules, time lengths, etc. I just go until I've exhausted the idea.

After a while I get the idea in full song form, and I perform it many times into the tape recorder and make small or large changes until it's completed. Knowing when it's finished is very important with my kind of writing because I make a new form every time. "Wonderful Baby" has a very different structure from "American Pie," and that is very different from "Tapestry," etc.

As you're working with your guitar, see how you can fit a new chord into a standard three-chord progression. When you find a new chord, it shakes your brain up for new melodic ideas. Just keep singing into your tape recorder, and listen back to find the moments of inspiration.

The Melodic Journey

Steve Seskin

Melody writing is far more mysterious than lyric writing. It's not as tangible and, therefore, harder to talk about. I write melodies for lyrics, so most of my notions about music center around how the melody fits the lyrics of each particular song. This concept is known as prosody (the marriage of lyrics and music). Prosody is important both in an overall sense and at every juncture of the song. How well the melody serves the lyrics in each passage affects whether the vibe or mood is right and whether the melody milks all the emotion out of the lyrics. A set of words can be completely redefined by adding different melodies to it.

There are numerous examples of great prosody. The melody of "Over the Rainbow," for example, puts the listener in a longing mode—looking to the sky for answers—right from the opening notes. In the classic Beatles' song "Yesterday," the reflective nature of the lyric and lament are brilliantly captured by the music. The melody of Bonnie Raitt's hit song "I Can't Make You Love Me" conveys both the lyric's hopelessness and the singer's resignation to how things are going to be.

THE RULE OF TWOS

Everything you do melodically is defined by what comes before it and what follows it. You should establish a melodic figure that interests the listener and then, at some point, go away from it to another passage that, by its nature, will make the listener want to hear the first figure again.

There are many notable exceptions to what's known as the "rule of twos," but I believe it usually works. This rule says that if you have completed a melodic figure (usually a line or less), you have a choice—to repeat it or not. If you don't repeat your first figure, you can follow it with something else, and then either repeat the first pattern or do something different again. The verse melody of "Over the Rainbow" has no repetitive patterns, but most pop, country, and contemporary folk music uses a lot of repetition. If you do choose to repeat your first melodic figure, your third figure should be something else that makes the listener long to hear that first figure again. Think of it this way. A beautiful melody is born. The listener is happy to hear it again. If you do it a third time, your brilliant melody becomes boring in a hurry. If you go somewhere else and then come back to it, it usually works better. In some songs, a melodic figure is established, repeated, and then starts a third time as a variation of the first two or in such a way that the ending of the phrase leads into the next section.

The rule of twos should also be respected in each section. In general, if you sing a verse, then repeat it, it's time to do something else. In "Over the Rainbow," when you hear the first verse, you're happy to hear the second verse. If they had done it a third time in a row, you would have hated the writers. Now, think of the bridge. The movement is quite different from the verse. It's not a coincidence. By the time the bridge is over, you're dying to hear the verse melody again. This is the mark of a classic melodic journey.

SECTION BY SECTION

If your songs are going to be melodically satisfying, you must look at specific parts of each song to see if the melody is doing its job. You should make sure that the sections in your songs—verse, chorus, bridge—are not too similar. For example, if you have a wordy verse, you should structure your chorus so it has fewer words and more long notes.

EMPHASIZE THE KEY WORDS

There is a word (or two) in every sentence that should get more emphasis than the others. Look at how you would say the line if you were speaking it, and let the melody reflect that. There's a line in an old song of mine that goes, "I used to be the king of wasted time." The original melody emphasized the word *be,* but I changed it so the emphasis was on *used.* This way the listener understands that the singer is no longer the king of wasted time. Think of melody as punctuation—a tool to lead the listener down the road we want them to go down. Don't understimate the power of the rest. Sometimes beats of silence can turn an ordinary passage into a poignant moment.

MELODIC TOOLS

There are four main tools that will help you to keep your melodies interesting: range, rhythm, syllabic content, and chordal background. You can use any or all of them. Look at the range of notes in the verse, and when you write the chorus, try to avoid the same melodic territory as the verse. You can overlap a bit, but leave yourself somewhere to go. If your chorus features a high D or E, save that moment. Don't use either of those notes in the verse. Most often, verse melodies are lower than the chorus—they lead up to it. But this is not an absolute. All the rules of songwriting are meant to be broken.

As for rhythm and syllabic content, don't use the same motif throughout the song. If both your verse and chorus are on the busy side, make sure the movement of the melody is different. In other words, the accents should fall in different places.

Let's talk about chords and chordal rhythms. The same notes can sound completely different depending on the chords you're playing and their movement. Try this with just one note. Sing a G note against a G-major chord, then move to an E minor, then a C, then a D, then an A minor, etc. The notes sound different against each one of these chords. Some of the best songs employ a simple melody with a changing chord pattern underneath it. You can also try the opposite approach and use a lot of notes to create a complex melody against one or two chords. The old R&B classic "Just My Imagination" features two chords for the whole song, yet it achieves a great melodic journey. The writers used range and rhythm to accomplish this. The listener doesn't even realize there are only two chords.

The rhythmic patterns under a melody can greatly alter the listener's perception of a piece of music. Are the chords being "pushed" or played on the beat? Is the drummer playing half-time or hitting the snare on all four beats of the measure?

PLAY WITH POSSIBILITIES

As a writer, your best friend is experimentation. Try a lot of things. If I'm happy with my chord progression, it's not unusual for me to fill up a tape with possibilities for a particular cadence in the song. If I go through my melodic choices and I'm still not happy, it's usually time to change my chordal pattern.

Here are some ways to shake things up with your melodies. Write without your instrument. Sing a melody into a Walkman, and then put chords to it, rather than letting the chords dictate the melody. Use a drum machine. These days you can get a great one for around $125, and it can really open you up rhythmically. Analyze which beat in the measure you usually start your melodies on. We all have our tendencies. Try something different. If you're prone to coming in on beat one, wait a beat or two.

Most of all, whether you're writing lyrics or melody, enjoy yourself. Celebrate your songwriting triumphs. Whether or not you're trying to sell your songs, make sure you get an intrinsic reward out of the process of writing them.

Lyric Lessons

Sam Shaber

Writing about songwriting is almost as tough as songwriting itself. How do you describe a process that is so intangible, so unformulaic, so undefined? Each song establishes its own set of rules and thus a framework to build around, and songwriting is also a very personal process—not because you have to reveal your most intimate thoughts to write a good song, but because your best tool is yourself and your experiences. This chapter will take you through the building of one of my own songs from beginning to end, drawing some lessons from my trials and tribulations.

Keep in mind that our focus here is not on writing songs that sell or following pop or country formulas where every song needs a chorus and many songs work around twists of phrase and poignant humor. Instead, we are just concerned with the broader *craft* of writing songs with a special focus on lyrics. The selling should come later.

GETTING STARTED

To write a song, the first thing you need is not an instrument or a voice or a tape recorder or a notebook. The first thing you need is an idea. This may sound overly simple, but it's truly the hardest part of the process. In this idea you must find many things, including musical genre, style, and the voice that will be communicating the song. Is it third person, first person, even second person (common in socially or politically directed songs)? Who's singing the lyrics? Is it you or a character? Will the voice use working-class slang, casual speech, or layered poetry? Are you going to lay the idea out on the table directly or will you use metaphor to communicate?

Please note that all of these answers do not have to be found right away, and in fact too much preparation can stunt your song's growth. If you let yourself get too tangled up in the who, what, where, when, and why of the song, chances are you will decide before you've even played a note that the idea has already been done or that it will never work.

I used to intellectualize my songwriting to an extreme degree—aiming for *Crime and Punishment* in each stanza. I'm not saying these songs were bad, but a wonderful thing happened when I let up a bit and let the emotions of the ideas come to me. Some of the strongest songs are written in 20 minutes with some adjustments after the fact. This is because the writer is letting the song go where it wants to, thus serving the music and the lyric at the same time.

Then there are songs that can take weeks or even months to complete. Sometimes this is because these tunes are fighting themselves: the music and the lyric don't fit together and there are roadblocks everywhere. When you're writing, you want to constantly let your mind go, so the ideas can work themselves out. Of course, few songs happen in one sitting, but if you find yourself struggling for weeks, be prepared to let go of something. Put the pieces away, and you might find that you can use them in future songs. I've thrown away an entire song and then dug up one line later to use in something completely different.

The concept of fooling around with words is key in lyric writing. It's a great help if you test things out, experiment a little, "audition" phrases and words and then possibly throw them away. There is no right or wrong, but there can be strong and weak choices.

You may be feeling "I love you so much, I can't live without you," but how can you express that in a way that hasn't been said a thousand times? The best way to find out is to fool around with the words, the feelings, the details. Who do you love? What are his or her traits, idiosyncrasies? If it's a man, does he make you laugh? Is he smart? Is he sexy? Could you think about how great it would be to live with him rather than how awful it would be to live without him? Can you describe your love from one particular moment of being together? Was there a second when you knew this was the one for you? What happened in that second?

INSIDE A SONG

Let's see how some of these concepts played out in the writing of my song "Honey" (from the album *perfecT* on Brown Chair Records). In this case, the idea was extremely simple. I was putting new strings on my guitar and listening to the standard tuning ring out as I warmed them up. I began to wonder if it would be possible to write a song using the open standard tuning as the main musical theme. So I let this open tuning ring out one string at a time—E A D G B E—and felt the darkness and the sadness of that combination. How long would they ring? How long would I wait? Would there ever be resolution?

This all sounds corny on paper, but I now had my vibe, and I wanted to pursue it. I began to think about a close friend of mine who was battling alcoholism—physically and emotionally, he needed the one thing that could really hurt him. And from this thought, together with the open strings, I came up with the line, "I will tip the neck of this bottle 'til it's coming out my eyes."

Boy, was I proud of myself for that one! What a line, I thought. I am a genius. The alcohol pours in and the tears pour out. Sheer poetry. A big note here is that sometimes when you find a line that you become very attached to, the first trick is to throw it away. It can only stunt the song's growth, especially if you are fixated on it. You have to be able to let go of things for the greater good of the song. It so happens that I kept this one in the end, but as the saying goes, "Do as I say, not as I do."

So I had this great line, but that was only the beginning of my problems. Now I had to figure out what to say about alcoholism. I had taken the voice of the alcoholic in that line, and now the alcoholic had to speak and finish the song. But I was fighting what was natural instead of going with the age-old advice to "write what you know." Not everyone sticks to this theory, and

---

FINDING A LYRICAL HOOK

To me, the best lyrics combine concrete images that set a scene with emotion that makes the listener care about the characters. A lyric has more impact if it has both of those things, as opposed to just being an emotional statement or just a scene-setting statement. An example is the song "I Can't Make You Love Me," which Bonnie Raitt recorded. It starts with, "Turn down the lights, turn down the bed / Turn down these voices inside my head." Those first two images give you a lot of information—they set the scene and tell you where you are; they tell you the time of day. But, the third line, "Turn down these voices inside my head," is the emotional statement that makes the listener care about what's going on.

Another example is an old Gordon Lightfoot song, "Second Cup of Coffee," that starts with, "I'm on my second cup of coffee and I still can't face the day." There again the image is the "second cup of coffee," which is a great image because you know that it's morning without saying, "It's seven in the morning." The image tells you the setting and the time and the place. But then "I still can't face the day" is what makes you want to hear more; it makes you wonder what's going on.

It's also important for writers to understand that they don't only have to write about their own lives. Obviously, writing about your own experiences is a good place to start, but if you want to become a more prolific writer and not run into writer's block all the time, it's important to write about other things. The notion is that you have an opinion about everything that happens that you hear about. In other words, if something happens to somebody else, you still have your own take on that. It's just as valid to write about that as about something that happened to you. And, along the same lines, it's just as valid to write about how you wish your life were as opposed to how it really is. For instance, if you had an unhappy childhood but you always had thoughts about what it would be like to be happy, you have a lot of visions of what a happy childhood would be like to draw upon. Just because you didn't have one doesn't mean that you can't write a song about how you wished it were. Those are a few things that free you up to write about stuff when your life is not going on one extreme or the other—joy or sorrow. You can always find something to write about if you look a little further than your own life.

—*Steve Seskin*

many people do very well writing about topics that interest them yet are very separate from their own experience, but I have never been able to do this.

Even the Broadway composers of the first half of the 1900s wrote largely what they knew. Johnny Mercer based the timeless tune "Moon River" on the actual Back River that runs by his old home on Burnside Island near Savannah, Georgia. And the greatest song-writers of our younger history—Joni Mitchell, Bob Dylan, Bruce Springsteen, Stevie Wonder—all tend to write what is intimate to them, whether playing a part or personally musing. Mitchell's "Amelia" rings with the conflict between life on the road and home-sickness, and when she sings, "I pulled into the Cactus Tree Motel to shower off the dust / And I slept on the strange pillows of my wanderlust," there she is, right in the lyric. The same is true for Stevie Wonder in a very different way. His personality lies more in the music and rhythm of the song—we feel like we know him because the energy and melody of the song are an expression of his own personal energy.

So back to a lowly songwriter in her living room with one decent line and not much else. How was I going to move into the mind of an alcoholic? I struggled with this and tried many different angles, deciding to work with the sense of defeat that can accom-pany addiction. This train of thought led to the original first verse:

> *Well I'm no poet, no lyric lines*
> *I just polish my defenses 'til they shine*
> *Can't write no love song, won't sing no lies*
> *But I will tip the neck of this bottle*
> *'Til it's coming out my eyes*

I didn't hate this, but I definitely didn't love it either. And where would I go from here? I didn't like the slang, and there just wasn't enough of me in it.

Then I listened again to those open, dissonant strings and found myself thinking about the loss of a friend in a car accident during a recent road trip. That was the idea that wanted to leave my head and wind up on paper. I started to hear the passage of time in those ringing notes, the life of memory. I also started to think about the places we vis-ited on the trip—some of them wide open spaces where winds begin at one end of the earth and you hear them whistling slowly all the way to the other side. We spent nights camping under the expanse of a Wyoming sky. We stayed in a leaky yurt on a friend's land in the New Mexico desert. We laughed a lot and took tons of pictures. And then after only ten days of what would have been a three-week trip, we got into a freak car accident from which I emerged practically unscathed and my friend never recovered.

This sudden turn of events has changed my life immensely, and it has also shown me how the same memory can be flavored in very different ways. Good times are recalled very differently when the person you shared them with is no longer around. And I decided not to be specific about the death, but to leave that detail up to the listener and focus on that longing, that sadness embedded in those open strings. After awhile, I had a semblance of the first verse:

> *Nighttime New Mexico*
> *Hard wept summer skies*
> *I danced to your heartbeat*
> *As we cuddled to stay dry*
> *You called me "Honey"*
> *Spoke in lullabies*
> *And now I tip the neck of this bottle*
> *'Til it's coming out my eyes*

Now I had the beginnings of a completely different song, but I was still able to keep my favorite line. The setup of the scene was very positive and then the last line of the stanza revealed that we are talking about a very painful experience. It's somewhat sudden for the listener, just as the sad events of my trip were sudden to me.

This is not the final incarnation of that verse—I eventually did some tweaking in the revision stage. It's not a good idea to get caught up in revision as you go—you will find yourself moving back two steps every time you move forward three. You can run out of steam this way. But let me jump ahead and explain what tweaking I later did and why.

The word *coming* was giving me trouble, as it sounded like the *bottle* was coming out my eyes instead of the tears. I changed it to *pouring,* which made the image more clear. I also squirmed at the verb *cuddled,* feeling it too cute for the tone of the song. There were a few other sore points that I sorted out to eventually arrive at:

Nighttime New Mexico
Flooding summer skies
I danced to your heartbeat
Pressing close to stay dry
You called me "Honey"
Spoke in lullabies
And now I tip the neck of this bottle
'Til it's pouring out my eyes

Now I was facing the chorus. Since the open strings on the verse were so lingering and uncontained, I decided to build this chorus section with very specific chordal and rhythmic borders. I based the lyric on part of a poem by Daniel Javitch, who had also been close to the friend I lost. The lines, which were not continuous in his poem, were "We shaped the hollows" and "I try to replicate the tone in everyone with yellow hair."

From these two lines, and with a simple Em, C, Em, C, B7 progression, I came up with:

We shaped the hollows
Placed our laughter there
And now I try to replicate the tone
In everyone with yellow hair

The word *replicate* is a bit awkward there, but my excuse was that the situation of seeing a deceased loved one in the faces and hair of strangers was a very sad, awkward image. And I loved the double meaning of the word *tone* in this context—sound and color. It also moved the time frame of the song from the memory of the person to the present tense, the aftermath, the lingering emotion.

In many ways, the hard part was now done. The first verse and chorus of a song set up the tone, the lyric structure, and the rhyme scheme, if any, and you can now paint by numbers a little bit.

I decided the second verse would move through more of the road trip:

Blue dawn in Yellowstone
Your breath even by my side
To be with you all over again
Again I'd drive all night
You called me "Honey"
Under Sweetwater skies
And now I tip the neck of this bottle
'Til it's pouring out my eyes

There is a little bit of alliteration—repetition of consonants—happening here, which I like to use in moderation. Some alliteration in your lyrics gives them their own personality and keeps the listener paying attention. Think of John Hiatt's great line "Memphis in the meantime, baby." Not only does it jump out at the listener and stick in your ear, but it's really fun to sing. In these verses I used simple pairs such as "nighttime New Mexico" and "Sweetwater skies." The repetition of words can also be interesting to fool around with, such as in "To be with you all over again / Again I'd drive all night."

Now I had these two verses and I was on my way. But I wanted to create an alternate line of thought in the song, both musically and lyrically. A bridge.

In building the bridge I again went with the idea of straightforward chords and rhythm, this time with a major-chord positive vibe. And lyrically, I decided to get even more specific with the details—as though we are now flipping through the happy pictures from the trip. The turn of events happens again, however, and the major chords turn back to minor at the end of the bridge. My first draft was this:

We scaled the wall to swim the waters
And shared in renegade smiles
And pitched our tent by restricted streambeds
Where we whispered secrets all night
We had a breakdown in Montana become a picnic spot
We had alleyways of Laramie beside the railroad lots
We had a view from Flagstaff of the Rockies stretching on and on and on
But where's my silver lining now that you are gone?

When I later went back and revised the song, the first half of the bridge wound up on the cutting-room floor, and I arrived at:

A breakdown in Montana became a picnic spot
Alleyways of Laramie beside the railroad lots
A view of the Rockies stretching on and on and on and on and on
But where's my silver lining now that you are gone?

Once I had made my way through the bridge, it was time to write that final verse and call it a day. I had traveled from New Mexico through Yellowstone, Sweetwater, Laramie, Boulder, Missoula, and now I wanted to return to that initial moment when the song and the memory began. In many story songs like this, the writer ends up in a very different place from where he or she began, but I wanted to find closure back in that desert:

New day, New Mexico
Coffee in the sun
Could I have known by that Taos mountain
That you would be the one?
You brought me honey
Warmed me inside
And now I'll tip the neck of this bottle
'Til it's pouring out my eyes

Of course the line "You would be the one" refers to the fact that my friend was the one who died later in the car accident, but rather than slamming that element over listeners' heads, I decided to leave it vague. Sometimes, the more possibilities available to the audience, the better. Universality is a great asset to any song, and this could easily be a story about a lover breaking things off after a romantic vacation.

Think about "Flowers for Zoe," by Lenny Kravitz, or the classic "Ode to Billie Joe," by Bobby Gentry, which leave quite a bit to our imagination. Kravitz is writing a ballad for his daughter as romantic and embracing as any love song, and "Ode to Billie Joe" slyly confronts us with a riddle, returning repeatedly to a choruslike progression with slightly different information in the lyric to keep the story moving. The mystery of that song has kept many a listener coming back and is one reason the song has been covered by so many different artists.

YOUR TURN

"Honey" is only one song, with one intent, one vibe, one story. There are as many different types of songs as there are songwriters.

Find your intent and your idea, and then find your guitar, your tape recorder, and your notebook and go to town. Just remember that it may not come easy, and even once the song is put together, sometimes taking a break from it and coming back to do revisions is the essential final step. No song is complete the first time through. It isn't just about having all the elements in place—a big part of the joy (and sweat) of songwriting is the fine tuning and reworking of a piece until you feel it is in its strongest form.

Whatever your musical style, always demand the freshest, most original writing from yourself. Don't get lazy and pick the easy way out lyrically. This is not to say that you should overcomplicate things—simple can be just as original as complex. To illustrate this, I want to close with a sample lyric from one of my favorite songwriters, Brooklyn-based Chris Moore. In an honest song about a blue-collar boy's crush on a wealthy girl in town ("Single Stroke," recorded on *Outa State Plates,* Real Deluxe Recordings), Moore writes:

> *I'll watch and wonder*
> *Let my imagination flow*
> *She don't break for lunch*
> *Or take five minutes to smoke*
> *She paints her masterpiece*
> *In a single stroke*

The lyrics are so simple yet so expressive that Moore touches me as a listener even though I'm not from the blue-collar town or inside the big mansion gate, and I think that is the greatest goal for any songwriter. Freshness, intelligence, and universality. No sweat, right?

Songwriting Traps and How to Avoid Them

Jamie Anderson

The songwriting muse, fueled by sheer emotion, just bestowed upon you a great song, and it feels nearly perfect. Sometimes the songwriting goddess is kind and you do get that wonderful tune right off the bat, but most often it's a good idea to take a second look at your perfect jewel. There are a lot of great songwriters and songs out there these days. Why should an audience be interested in yours? Most songwriters fall into similar traps, so here are some tips for making your songs more compelling and keeping your audience interested.

AVOID CLICHES

"You're every beat of my heart." "I'll love you forever." So what? If a bazillion other songwriters have used the same words, why would listeners want to hear it from you too? Find a fresh way to say the same thing. Do your best to rid the world of those evil clichés, but don't worry if one slips in once in a while. One well-placed cliché can act like a good hook, because it provides a place for the listener's ear to rest. But too many clichés will make you sound like a bad '70s pop band.

EXPLORE OTHER TIME SIGNATURES

We all love 4/4. Heck, almost every rock song on the planet is in 4/4. But like Mom used to say, if everyone jumps off the 4/4 cliff, does that mean you should also? See what 3/4 time does to a sad ballad. Or how 7/8 spices up that jazzy folk tune. If you're not sure how to discover other time signatures, try playing along with your favorite CDs. Don't worry about getting all the chords right, just concentrate on the feel and the time. Pretty soon, these other grooves will creep into your cells, and the next time the muse calls, you will be taking a detour around that 4/4 jump-off.

KEEP IT MOVING

Does the story in your song have a beginning, middle, and end? Does the plot have an interesting twist? Or some kind of resolution? If your focus is on descriptive phrases that don't actively portray a direction, the words have to be extremely compelling. It might be easier to rethink your plot and give the story some movement. Have the characters do something besides fall in love and break up. Or if they do break up, have the reason be that one wears ugly ties and the other is obsessed with Jerry Springer. OK, that's a *little* far out, so try looking at the people around you to get ideas. Why have their relationships ended? Use your own life as an example, and don't hold back on the emotion, because it can really drive a song.

WRITE WHAT YOU KNOW

It's the advice given by many writing experts, whether you're writing a novel or a song. But don't feel like you have to write everything as it happened. If you've broken up with your beloved because she doesn't like your ties, you don't have to tell every detail of the breakup. Go ahead and barf out the entire tale when you first start writing, but edit ruthlessly later, so that you have a song without too many main ideas. I know a songwriting teacher who tells her students to write no more than three verses and a chorus—or two verses, a bridge, and a chorus. It's good advice. If you can't fit the story into that format, you probably have too much information. Of course, there are some exceptions to this rule—witness some of those long folk ballads—but don't make every one of your songs a multilevel train wreck. Give them a clear track to follow.

KEEP IT SIMPLE

Can listeners follow your story? Do they laugh at the funny lines? Get teary at the sad ones? Clap enthusiastically when the song ends? If not, look at how you've presented the tale. If you're using a complicated melody to present a detailed plot, the words may be lost in the music. Try streamlining your complicated tale with a simpler melody. Cut out a few of those eighth notes and add some rests. Try playing a new set of chords altogether. And yes, I know I suggested trying different time signatures, but if you're telling a story rich with detail, you may want to use 4/4 or 3/4 so the lyrics aren't lost in an odd beat.

SHOW, DON'T TELL

You may be losing the audience because you've told them what to feel. Don't declare, "I'm sad you left me." Try saying, "The mournful sound of a faraway train whistle makes me think of you." You want to make an audience feel a certain way but you've got to sneak up on them.

GET SPECIFIC

You can put a kick in your lyrics by using descriptive words. A thesaurus is a great tool. Get rid of those boring verbs! Instead of *walk,* try *saunter* or *stroll.* Likewise with adjectives. Instead of *loud noise,* try *screech* or *clank.* Use all your senses. How does it smell? Taste? Feel? It also helps to be specific with brand names and people's names. Instead of *car,* say *Corvette,* instead of *brother,* say *Bobby.* Imagine you've written a line like "She went to the store to buy a loaf of bread." Try adding specific verbs and adjectives to make it more interesting. How about, "Ellen raced into the A&P to buy the last of the sweet-smelling cinnamon bread." Now your listener wants to know who Ellen is, why she was in a hurry, and why it was the last loaf of bread. Before that, she was just an anonymous woman in a no-name store.

EXPAND YOUR CHORDAL VOCABULARY

I–IV–V is a common chord progression. It's been used by everyone from the Beatles to Cheryl Wheeler, so it's OK for you to use, right? Sure. Listeners sometimes like that familiar pattern, so it's not a crime to use it. But you may want to consider spicing it up. Instead of C, F, G7, try C, Dm, Gmaj7. Or throw in a transitional chord like Am between the C and F. Better yet, make that an Am7. And even better than that, find new ways to play those chords. There are many ways to play a G chord, and if you play it higher up the neck than the usual open position, it may free up new melodic possibilities for you. Or, take that G chord and give it a different bass note. Even if you're still singing the same melody you had when you were playing C, F, G7, this new chord progression could add interest to an otherwise run-of-the-mill song.

LOOK OUT FOR THE BRIDGE

A common mistake is to have a bridge when one isn't needed. A bridge should offer new information and usually has a different melody or feel. If you're not introducing new information, consider making the bridge another verse or eliminating it all together.

MAKE THE CHORUS STAND OUT

Make sure there's enough melodic and harmonic contrast between the verse and the chorus. It's tempting to just use the chords you can easily play when you write, but if you use the same chords for the verse and the chorus, chances are good that the melodies are going to sound alike. You can look at your lyric sheet and know the difference, but will your listeners? Think about starting the chorus with a different chord than the verse. Make an effort to use a completely different chord progression, one that will encourage a different melody or feel.

DON'T GIVE AWAY THE GOODS TOO SOON

Where is the highest note? The most poignant line? The funniest lyric? The most dynamic rhythm? If these fall in an odd place—at the start of a verse, for example—then the effect will be diminished. Peaks of interest are most often in the chorus or toward the end of a song.

GET FEEDBACK

Listener responses will tell you a lot about which aspects of your songs are working and which need work. An audience can give you feedback, but you should also play your songs for other songwriters, family members, friends, and strangers in the street.

Now go back to that great song and make it better!

Thanks to Bernice Lewis, Dave Nachmanoff, and Kiya Heartwood for their suggestions.

Editing Your Songs

Jeffrey Pepper Rodgers

We all love those songs that come fast and whole. Like a baby born in a taxicab, they seem to know exactly what to do and what they're about, and our job is mostly just to catch them before they fall. And when they're spanking new in our hands, they feel so complete and *right,* a mood or emotion or thought miraculously made flesh. Any tinkering would only dilute their effect.

In reality, though, relatively few songs (and relatively few babies) come into being this way—most require time and labor. For many songwriters, myself included, this is a hard truth to swallow. Finding inspiration, or letting it find you, is the essential beginning of the process, but it's equally important to develop the ability to be a song editor—to identify what needs trimming and what needs expanding, what's essential and what's just taking up space, and, of course, to have the courage to act on your findings. In my own case, what really developed my eyes/ear as a song editor (much to the chagrin of the side of me that greatly preferred the crank-'em-out-and-move-on method) was becoming a professional magazine and book editor. In that field, I learned to identify the weak spots (and strengths) in other people's writing and to work with and around them, and those skills quickly translated to editing my own words. In time, a similar process took hold in my songwriting, which slowed my output but raised its quality several notches.

Editing can be a very different process in different situations, but let's talk about some common weaknesses in writing and how you can address them to make the idea at the core of your song really shine. Note that all of the following applies equally to lyrics, melody, instrumental riffs, chord progressions—all the parts that contribute to your song's mood and meaning.

YOUR FAVORITE THINGS

In many songs, there's one detail that you really, really love—a line or a lick or a chord change that gives you intense pleasure. Now, this little detail could, in fact, be central to your song and give your listeners the same charge that it gives you, and if so, you certainly don't want to touch it. But you need to assess this detail carefully, especially if it's something that has been hanging around for a long time, awaiting a home. When you have favorite things like this, the desire to show the world your brilliant notion can definitely cloud your judgment about what really belongs in a song. I personally am prone to developing unhealthy attachments to cool little guitar licks or chord moves, which I'll play incessantly for months and even years, and I'll do anything to shoehorn them into a work in progress.

In the heat of creating, it's not always easy to separate the things that fit from the things that are desperately trying to hitch a ride with your song. When you've got some distance from it (usually in a subsequent writing session, after a break), listen closely to how the song flows into and away from this moment. Are you awkwardly veering in a new direction or mood? Assuming a different idiom, voice, or point of view? Does arriving at or departing from this moment require a lengthy transition, most of which just performs a setup or tear-down function rather than contributing something to the song in itself? A positive answer to any of these questions is a sign that you may be trying to squeeze in something extraneous, or at least that you need to improve your transitions.

FLYING ON AUTOPILOT

During the writing process, there are times when you are very much in charge, and others where you fill in a line/lick/chord just because you've so often heard it done that way—it's like temporarily leaving the cockpit and letting autopilot take over. When you do this, what you wind up with in your song is a cliché, which isn't necessarily a bad thing, but it *is* bad if your listeners are so familiar with the cliché that their ears and attention shut down when they hear it. The first time someone sang, "I don't know where I'm going, but I sure know where I've been," the lines may have had some resonance, but now . . .

If, while you're in editing mode, you come across a detail that's a little too familiar—so much so that it doesn't really sound as if you wrote it—there are a few approaches you can take. One, of course, is just to replace the whole thing with an original expression, which is great if you can pull it off. But it can also be equally effective, or even more effective, to play off the cliché: to tweak it a little bit, whether by substituting a word or syncopating a riff differently or introducing whatever variation works in your context. This way, your listeners get that nice feeling of familiarity from the cliché along with the extra nice feeling of having their expectations toyed with a little bit, which is one of the best tricks in the songwriter's bag. I'm just riffing here, but if you changed that line to "I don't know where I'm going, but I sure know where *you've* been," you've created some juicy new possibilities.

Some songwriters play with clichés on a grand scale. Take an example from the witty songbook of Jill Sobule: Her song "Love Is Never Equal" takes its form from the old country-crooner duet, but as the title implies, she substitutes a cynical, funny message for the usual sap. Then, in the studio, she extended the mischief by enlisting the king of anti-Nashville country, Steve Earle, to harmonize with her and deliver lines like "Someone always gets kicked to the curb" and by asking all the musicians to play in a "sloppy, bar-like" way. The result not only skewers the cliché but delivers a delicious alternative to the typical breakup song.

MAKING MORE FROM LESS

With words (prose or lyrics), it's extremely common for writers to pile on adjectives, adverbs, and other descriptors in a noble, gallant, and well-intentioned effort to be vivid. The problem is that these words start to cancel each other out, and the whole effect is lost. The same thing can happen with musical details (even whole verses or sections of songs), and some judicious pruning can make a big difference in your song's impact. If you have a pile of similar words, pick the one that best expresses the most important idea and clear out the rest. If there isn't a single word weighty enough to do the job by itself, keep pushing until you find one that can. Also remember that a good, concrete image trumps *any* sort of description. Jill Sobule could have explained to us that affairs always end with someone feeling hurt and discarded, but how would that have compared with seeing someone get "kicked to the curb"? Ouch.

Not all songs need to be short and sparse—long, extravagant, and involved songs can be beautiful things. But in all songs, regardless of the size or scope, everything must contribute to the whole, and your job as an editor is to understand what exactly that "whole" is and identify what advances the cause and what doesn't. Some writers need to spin out ten verses in order to pare back to the four that really count, while others just keep on polishing the same four. There's no "correct" editing process, just a result that's either tightly constructed or not quite.

As you flesh out your ideas, you should be sure not to overlook the materials you've already got in hand. Try extending an existing image, returning to the opening scene, embellishing the intro guitar riff or transferring it to another chord. Building on what you've already written serves several purposes: it makes the song more coherent, it helps you avoid mixing metaphors and other internal clashes, and it sets up a resonance inside the song, so that listeners will settle in with an idea and then feel it being changed. This technique is similar to modifying a cliché, except you're setting up your own familiar pattern and then playing with it.

FOLLOWING THE ARC

Every song is a story, which starts somewhere, heads off on a little journey, and winds up someplace else. In editing, you should think about your song in this light, whether or not it has action or a plot—even a mood song should be a journey, maybe further into or out of that mood.

Take a look at what people in the publishing business call the lead—your opening music and words. Generally speaking, the song form is extremely condensed, and you don't want people to have to wait to get to the good stuff. In editing prose, I often find that writers bury a great lead several paragraphs in, and that the original opening material fits in perfectly later in the piece. Songwriters sometimes do the same thing, and while you shouldn't feel pressured to dazzle your audience with your lead, you want to make sure to start drawing them in right away. At the moment, I've got this Greg Brown song stuck in my head that opens with an ominous minor-chord strum and this line delivered in his amazing rumble of a voice: "So how are things going in the small dark movie of your life?" So much information and intrigue is packed in that image (again, it's an image and not description) that I *have* to know more.

After the lead, pay attention to how the song develops through the middle and the end. I've noticed that in my weaker songs, such microscopic changes occur from beginning to end that I am assuming way too much of listeners. There's just no getting around it: unless you happen to be Bob Dylan, other people are not as attuned to the nuances of your songs (or at least not to the same nuances) as you are. Try to put yourself in their position and think about where they are being taken in the four-minute journey. You have to provide them with a reason to want to go from verse one to verse two and on through the chorus to the end. To continue with the example of "Small Dark Movie," Greg Brown goes on to frame the sordid life suggested in the lead, using a different angle for each verse: from "Late at night you call your girlfriend / In the morning you call your wife" in the first verse to "You could really use a raincoat and a pair of cool shoes / You could really use some idea what it is you're trying to do" in the second to some scary road imagery in the third: "Change is a semi with smoking wheels filling the rearview mirror." A lonesome slide solo by Kelly Joe Phelps extends the mood and melody, and then Brown wraps up by returning to the first verse, which at this point has a whole new set of associations. As he fades out repeating "How are things going?" Brown also leaves us with the suspicion that the narrator might not really be talking to "you" at all, but to himself. That's a lot to chew on in a short, simple, chorusless song, and it stays with me even though I haven't spun that disc in weeks.

When you're pursuing a new inspiration, you could be lucky enough to arrive at a complete composition on your first pass, but more often than not you'll need to call on the services of your inner editor to get a song where it needs to go. No matter what techniques or approaches you're using, the secret of being a good editor is being able to view your song from the other side of the guitar. You want to know, what are listeners experiencing here? What do they want and need as the song develops? When you can answer those questions and deliver the goods, you're there. Congratulations. Enjoy your new song.

Expanding Your Chord Vocabulary

Gary Talley

Although songwriters like Hank Williams, Bob Dylan, and Harlan Howard have written many great three-chord songs, you should give yourself a few more options as a songwriter. Without getting too much into theory, I'd like to try to expand your chord knowledge in a practical and applicable way. What we want to achieve here is a stronger understanding of chords and chord progressions as used in popular music—well, all styles except classical and jazz, which are generally more harmonically complex.

When talking about chord progressions, I like to use the Nashville number system instead of words like *tonic, dominant,* and *subdominant.* The system has nothing to do with country music per se; it's useful in understanding any chord progression in any style of music.

THE ESSENTIAL CHORDS

The chart below shows the basic chords in five guitar-friendly keys: G, C, D, A, and E.

Key	Chords in the Five "Guitar Friendly" Keys					Connectors	
1	2m	3m	4	5^7	6	1/3	5/7
G	Am	Bm	C	D^7	Em	G/B	D/F♯
C	Dm	Em	F	G^7	Am	C/E	G/B
D	Em	F♯m	G	A^7	Bm	D/F♯	A/C♯
A	Bm	C♯m	D	E^7	F♯m	A/C♯	E/G♯
E	F♯m	G♯m	A	B^7	C♯m	E/G♯	B/D♯

The basic and most common chords in every key are 1, 2m, 3m, 4, $5^{(7)}$, and 6m. These chords are totally made up of the tones of the major scale of the 1 chord. For example, all the notes of all the chords in the key of G are made up entirely of the notes of the G-major scale (G A B C D E F♯ G). The C chord is called the 4 chord in the key of G because it is based on the fourth note of the G-major scale. The D chord is based on the fifth note of the G-major scale.

Let's look at the three most important chords in any key, the 1, 4, and 5 chords. The 1 chord, the tonic, is usually the last chord of the song. A chord progression tends to *resolve* back to the 1 chord. The 5 chord most often leads back to the 1 chord, especially if it is a seventh chord.

Pick up your guitar and play a D chord. Notice how it sounds static or final. It could be the last chord in a song. Now play a D7. Can you hear the *leading* sound that implies another chord is coming? The D7 is *setting up* the G chord. It's just like when you're singing "Jingle Bells" and someone hits a seventh chord (the 5^7) at the end of the verse while everyone sings "ohhhhh," then resolves to the 1 on "jingle bells."

So the two most necessary chords in a chord progression are the 1 and the 5^7. The 1 is the home chord you want to get back to, and the 5^7 chord leads you back there. If you hear a song with only two chords, you can bet they're going to be the 1 and the 5^7, as in "Jambalaya," "Tulsa Time," and "Achy Breaky Heart."

The next most common chord is the 4 chord. When you hear a three-chord song, it's almost always the 1, 4, and 5 chords. The 4 chord does not imply any motion, so it's a place to go after the 1 chord and before any other chord. You can also put a 5 chord *without* a seventh just about anywhere in the chord progression.

There are three minor chords common to every key: the 2m, 3m, and 6m. The 2m and 6m are the most common. The 2m often precedes the 5^7 chord, and it can also be substituted for the 4 chord because it is the relative minor of the 4 chord. The 6m is the relative minor of the 1 chord. It can be substituted for the 1, but usually not in the last measure of a verse or chorus. The 3m, the relative minor of the 5 chord, is not as common as the 2m or 6m, but it has a sound of its own. Good examples of what the 3m sounds like can be heard in "Early Morning Rain" by Gordon Lightfoot, "Smoky Mountain Rain" by Ronnie Milsap, and "Lay, Lady, Lay" by Bob Dylan.

If you count the 5 and 5^7 as two chords, that makes seven chords in five keys that are absolutely essential. That doesn't mean that you have to learn 35 chords, however, because some are duplicated. It actually comes out to 19 chords. With these 19 chords, you can rule the world!

CONNECTOR CHORDS

But let's not stop with those basic chords. You can add a little more variety in your songs by using two common connector chords: the 1/3 (1 over 3) and 5/7 (5 over 7). Here are several examples of these chords:

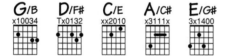

They have specific jobs to do in a chord progression, connecting the seven basic chords, so their use is very logical and predictable. Let's look at the 1/3 chord. It's always next to a 4 chord. Using the key of G as an example, the 1/3 chord would be a G/B. The top letter (or number) indicates the chord (G), and the bottom one stands for the bass note (or lowest note) of the chord (B, second fret, fifth string). If you'll look at the chord diagram, you'll see that it's just a G chord with a different bass note. The B note is already in the chord, so all you're doing is leaving out the usual G bass note.

If you're strumming a guitar in an undisciplined manner, hitting all the strings every time you strum, you won't be able to hear the difference between a G chord and a G/B. Play a G chord this way: hit the bass-note G (third fret, sixth string) by itself first, *then* strum the rest of the strings. Now, to play the G/B, hit the bass-note B (second fret, fifth string) and then strum. Now, do the same thing with a C chord: hit the C note (third fret, fifth string) first and then strum. Hitting the correct bass note is the key. In the G to G/B to C chord progression, you can hear the bass note *walk up* from G to B to C. Here's how that progression might lead back to the 1 chord:

G	G/B	C	D7	G
1	1/3	4	5^7	1

So any time you want to go from a 1 chord to a 4 chord, you can connect them with a 1/3. That's the first of the 1/3 chord's two jobs. The second job is connecting a 4 to a 2m. In the key of G, the progression would be C–G/B–Am, as in this example:

C	G/B	Am	D7	G
4	1/3	2m	5^7	1

Now for the 5/7 chord. This one's really easy. The 5/7 chord always connects a 1 chord to a 6m chord, no matter which comes first. So, in the key of G, it would be G–D/F♯–Em (1 to 5/7 to 6m) or Em–D/F♯–G (6m to 5/7 to 1).

ADDING COLOR

OK, now we've got our basic major and minor chords and we know how to connect them with our two connectors, but suppose we want to add more *color* or *texture* to our songs. The most important color chords are the add9 and sus4 chords. Let's start with the add9 chords. Using the key of G as an example, let's play a Gadd9:

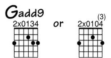

What we're doing is adding the A note (second fret, third string) to the G chord. (It's a 9 because it's nine scale tones up from the root G.) What would you call that sound? My students have said "open," "spacey," "wistful." Close intervals give it a certain character. You could play the A note on the top of the chord, but it wouldn't have the same effect. The add9's are best used on the 1 chord and 4 chord (or both). Remember, the add9's are options and will sound a little too modern for traditional music. Here are a few more examples of add9 chords:

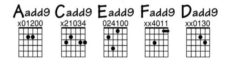

The other common color chord is the sus4. The one most people learn first is the Dsus4. Just add your pinky (third fret, first string) to a D chord. The "sus" means *suspended,* not sustained. The sus4 chord usually goes back to the major chord (Dsus4 to D) before it goes to the next chord. Sus4's are most common on the 5 chord (or 5⁷ chord). You can also use them on the 1 chord (especially in intros and verses on ballads and mid-tempo songs). Here are some other examples of sus4 chords:

If you want to add an edgy blues or rock sound to your songs, try these two chords: the ♭3 and the ♭7. In the key of G, they would be B♭ and F. Try them along with the 1, 4, and 5 chords (and go easy on the minors, connectors, and color chords).

DIMINISHED CHORDS

Now let's take a look at diminished chords, which are usually used as connector chords. There's one place in a chord progression where diminished chords are fairly common: to connect the 5 and 6m chords. For instance, in the key of G, you'd have a D chord, D♯° (sharp diminished), and an Em chord. The ♯5° (sharp five diminished) connects the D to the Em.

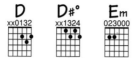

Examples of this can be found in "Mr. Bojangles" and "Wind beneath My Wings." Another, less common diminished chord is the $\sharp1^\circ$ (sharp one diminished) connecting a 1 to a 2m chord, as in this progression in G: G–G$\sharp^\circ$–Am. A common *turnaround* in a country swing or ragtime tune would be: 1–$\sharp1^\circ$–2m–5^7 (G–G$\sharp^\circ$–Am–D7).

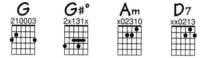

The only other diminished chord you're likely to find in popular music is the $\sharp4^\circ$ after a 4 chord in a blues or ragtime tune. The 1 chord usually follows, as in this example:

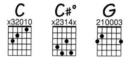

"Back to Louisiana," by Delbert McClinton, is a good example.

CHORD VOICINGS

Now that you've got the basics, let's talk about chord voicings. How you voice a chord can make a big difference. A major chord has only three tones (a triad), but on a guitar you have six strings. So when you play a six-note chord, you're always doubling some of those tones.

Try a G chord like this:

Now add your ring finger on the third fret, second string, to get this chord:

It's still a G chord, but with a different voicing. Now take your index finger off the B note (second fret, fifth string) and tilt your middle finger a little so that the fleshy part of your finger just touches the fifth string, thereby muting it. Now strum the chord. It's still a G chord, but it has no thirds (no B notes).

Now play a plain old G7 chord:

The seventh (F) is sitting right on top of the triad. This voicing doesn't work well in most of today's music. As a matter of fact, it always sounds a bit like a ukulele chord to me. Instead, try the chord like this, where the seventh is in the middle of the chord—it sounds much more balanced:

You can also walk down with the seventh (F), sixth (E), and fifth (D) on the fourth string, which sounds pretty cool.

Look at this Csus4 chord:

Leave your middle finger on the second fret, fourth string, because a sus4 chord almost always goes back to the basic chord. The thing to remember here is *not* to play the first string open, because you're adding back a third (E) to the chord, which you just took out when you added the 4 (F) with your pinky. So you're weakening the sus4 sound considerably by playing the high E string.

The first A7 chord below sounds ukulele-ish to me. Instead, try the A7 shape at right, which you can also move up to the fifth fret for another A7 voicing:

Here are a few ways to play a Cadd9. If you're already playing a C chord, you can make the first Cadd9 voicing by just adding the 9 with your pinky. The second chord sounds great after you play the G shown at right:

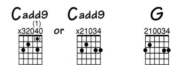

Every chord can be voiced in a wide variety of ways. I hope that the voicings covered in this workshop expand your horizons and begin to shake up your chord progressions.

Understanding Chord Progressions
Stephen Dick

PART ONE

A song is a balancing act. A songwriter strives to balance lyrics, rhythm, melody, and instrumental counterpoint to express an emotion or tell a story. These parts are held together by harmony, the chord changes the songwriter chooses to bind a song.

The essence of a song often lies in its chord changes. Know the changes, and you pretty much know the song. How is it that so much of a song, not just its structure but its heart, can be distilled down to a simple string of letters and symbols?

It's common to say that chords represent basic emotions. In grade school we're told that major chords are happy and minor chords are sad. Harmony, however, is more than the feelings evoked by single chords. The chords a songwriter chooses affect us in the way they play upon our expectations. Working with or against those expectations, a song's chords can soothe us with a comforting familiarity or upset us with a twisted logic.

These expectations develop early on. As children, we learn the basic sounds of our natal language by hearing our parents speak. We learn the essential features of our natal musical language in the same way, in the sounds that pour out to us from our mothers' lullabies and our dads' accordions, from cartoon theme songs, and, in another era, from school music programs.

Just as we begin to grasp the essential grammar of spoken language through repeated hearing and practice, we learn the essential grammar of music through repeated exposure and active involvement. Without necessarily ever articulating the idea, we come to understand that the basic workings of harmony remain the same, whether we're listening to Bach or the Beatles. Our intuitive understanding of music continues to evolve as long as we listen with the hungry ears of children.

The more we learn to appreciate the basic patterns of harmony, the more we appreciate it when those patterns are disturbed. Thus, a song's chords express something deeper than simple, fixed emotions like happiness or sadness. Rather, they express the kinds of feelings that can arise out of working against expectations, the complicated emotions of transformation, such as ambiguity, anticipation, defiance, loss, or desire. No wonder they're called *changes*.

FUNDAMENTAL MOVES

The basic functions of harmony in Western music are simple. With a thousand marvelous exceptions, they are:

V goes to I
IV goes to V or I
I goes to IV or V

CHORD NOTATION

Roman numerals are often used in jazz and classical music as a shorthand way of talking about chords. Each chord in a given key is assigned a number—uppercase for major chords and lowercase for minor or diminished chords. For example, here are the chords in the key of C:

I	ii	iii	IV	V	vi	vii
C	Dm	Em	F	G	Am	Bdim

In major keys, chords I, IV, and V are major chords; chords ii, iii, and vi are minor chords; and chord vii is a diminished chord.

In minor keys, chords i and iv are minor; chords III and V are major; and chords ii, vi, vii are diminished (or minor, or major, or augmented, depending on which minor mode you're using).

The suffixes used with standard chord symbols indicate any alterations to the basic, diatonic chord forms. Thus, the pattern

Cmaj7   Bm7♭5   FmMaj7   G9

would be written in the key of C as

Imaj7   vii7♭5   ivmaj7   V9

This system is very similar to the Nashville numbering system. Both systems allow you to move chord patterns around from key to key, provided you know where you left your keys.

(For a quick guide to the Roman numeral system for notating chords, see "Chord Notation.")

Of these three, "V goes to I" is the most essential. The sense of resolution we hear when we play I, then V, then I again (for example, C to G to C, D to A to D, or E to B to E) is one of the intuitions we develop about music from an early age. Although it can be explained in terms of physics or music theory, the most basic explanation is that we hear V resolve to I because that's what we're used to hearing. Those who grow up in other musical traditions hear other dissonances and resolutions.

You can hear this basic function at work in a song like Hank Williams' "Jambalaya." In the first line, I goes to V, and in the second, V goes to I (V7 is V, only more so). The symbol ⁒ indicates that you play the same chord from the previous measure.

| I | ⁒ | ⁒ | ⁒ | V7 | ⁒ | ⁒ | ⁒ |
| ⁒ | ⁒ | ⁒ | ⁒ | I | ⁒ | ⁒ | ⁒ |

Let's play with the three functions a little. Choose a minor key, use both versions of the third function (i goes to iv and i goes to V), add the first function (V goes to i), and you've got Santana's "Black Magic Woman":

i	⁒	v	⁒
i	⁒	iv	⁒
i	V	i	⁒

Put the same functions together a little differently and you've got the old lullaby "Hush-a-Bye (All the Pretty Little Horses)." In the first line ("Hush-a-bye, don't you cry"), i goes to iv. And in the second line ("Go to sleep you little baby"), i goes to V7 and then V7 goes to i.

| i | ⁒ | iv | ⁒ |
| i7 | V7 | i | ⁒ |

BASIC SUBSTITUTIONS

The remaining chords in a diatonic scale, ii, iii, vi, and vii, each have two notes in common with one of the three basic chords. This overlapping allows each of them to be substituted for one of those chords. Thus:

ii substitutes for IV
iii or vi substitute for I
vii substitutes for V

One chord can substitute for another either by replacing it entirely or by extending it a few extra measures, adding color to an otherwise static harmony.

A well-known and subtle example of extension by substitution is in the opening chords of "Eleanor Rigby," where Lennon and McCartney start on C and go to Em. What makes this simple opening so effective is its ambiguity. When we hear a song start in C, we expect it to be in the key of C major. When the Em comes in, we hear it at first as a substitution for C (iii substitutes for I). This is reinforced when the two-chord pattern is repeated. It's only after the introduction, when the verse starts, that we find we're actually in the key of E minor and that the substitution was actually VI (C) substituting for i (Em). This sense of not quite fitting in without actually being dissonant is a musical distillation of the lives described in the song.

A common pattern of substitution is to start with the basic pattern I–IV–V and then substitute vi for I and ii for IV, giving you the chords for "Heart and Soul" and a hundred other tunes. The first line has the straight I–IV–V pattern, then the second line has the substitutions of the vi and ii.

| I | ⁒ | IV | V |
| I | vi | ii | V |

This set of changes shows how the "V goes to I" function is central to standard Western music. If V is built on the fifth degree of the scale starting on I, then the "V of V" should be built on the fifth degree of the scale starting on V. Check it out in the diagram below: in the diatonic scheme of things, ii goes to V and vi goes to ii. This means that the "Heart and Soul" changes (I–vi–ii–V–I) are just a more elaborate illustration of the basic function "V goes to I."

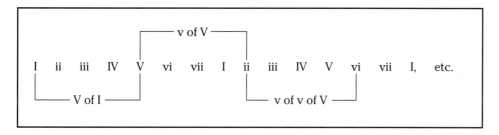

Let's have a little fun. Following this pattern, the chord that leads to vi would be iii (five steps up the scale, starting with vi). Thus, we could start with the opening to "Eleanor Rigby" and go on to build a song on:

| I | iii | vi | ii | V | I |
| C | Em | Am | Dm | G | C |

Now, let's spice things up by turning all those minor chords (and the V) into dominant seventh chords:

| C | E7 | A7 | D7 | G7 | C |

And, voilà, we have the basic changes to Willie Nelson's "On the Road Again" and a basic part of dozens of ragtime and swing tunes.

Once you get to know the basic moves, the "goes to" and the "substitutes for" patterns, you can go on stringing chord changes together indefinitely. Like the basic building blocks of DNA, these simple functions can be combined in an infinite number of ways to create new songs.

PART TWO

INSIDE A CLASSIC SONG

As a way of summing up what we've discussed so far, I'd like to focus on one song to see how a skilled songwriter, the late Townes Van Zandt, used these ideas to deepen simple lyrics with shades of meaning. Like Picasso conjuring up a bull with a few simple brush strokes, Van Zandt could create a world with a handful of well-placed chords.

One of Van Zandt's best-known songs is "Pancho and Lefty," which was a hit for Willie Nelson and Merle Haggard in 1983. You can hear Van Zandt's version on the Sugar Hill release *Rear View Mirror.* The song never drifts into maudlin melodrama, and it communicates a mood of simple resignation and offers a sort of left-handed benediction to losers. Every element of the song contributes to this mood, but the harmony holds it all together and sustains the mood throughout.

The changes seem simple at first. The chords under the opening lines ("Livin' on the road my friend / Was gonna keep you free and clean / But now you wear your skin like iron / And your breath's as hard as kerosene") are just I, IV, and V: C, F, and G in the key of C.

| I | ╱ | V | ╱ |
| IV | ╱ | I | V |

To see what's so unusual about this simple chord progression, take one more look at the first three principles I laid out in the beginning of this chapter:

V goes to I
IV goes to V or I
I goes to IV or V

The only combination of these three chords not mentioned is V goes to IV, and yet in the fourth and fifth measures of this song, Van Zandt had V going to IV. What gives?

There's a difference between one chord *resolving* to another and one chord *following* another. V doesn't resolve to IV. This creates a disconnection between the first four measures and the second four measures. It's what a composition teacher of mine used to call "one damned thing after another." Lyrically and harmonically, the two four-bar phrases are separate statements placed in contrast with each other.

There's also something pleasantly subversive going on. Take another look at the second four measures. Although they follow the rules, they do so in an odd way. IV goes to I and I goes to V, but they seem to be going in the wrong order. Generally, we would expect to hear IV–V–I or I–IV–V. As it is, things end rather unsatisfactorily on IV–I–V.

I think it says something about the quality of Van Zandt's writing that the same words used to describe the harmony could be used to describe the view of life expressed in the lyrics: "The changes seem simple at first, but it's one damned thing after another. There's something pleasantly subversive going on, but things end unsatisfactorily."

The same teacher who taught me that music sometimes sounds like one damned thing after another also taught me to look for what it is that holds such seemingly random music together. What holds "Pancho and Lefty" together is Van Zandt's masterful manipulation of a single, basic chord pattern: IV–I. Look at those first eight measures again and hear them as IV–I patterns in different keys:

IV–I in G
| C | ╱ | G | ╱ |
IV–I in C
| F | ╱ | C | G |

This emphasis on IV–I is underscored by the instrumental opening of the song, which rocks back and forth between I and IV for four measures.

In the next ten measures, Van Zandt took advantage of another set of basic principles we discussed before. To refresh your memory:

ii substitutes for IV
iii or vi substitutes for I
vii substitutes for V

To vary the basic IV–I pattern and to give the song more depth and color, Van Zandt used substitutions for one or the other of the chords in the IV–I pattern. Thus, in the next ten measures, IV–I becomes IV–vi or ii–I.

IV–I in C   IV–vi in C
                ii–I in G
| F | ⅋ | C | F | Am | G |
      IV–vi in C
| G | F | Am | ⅋ |

Something striking about these ten measures is that there are ten instead of eight. Generally, simple tunes tend to form simple patterns. Two-measure motifs join to form four-measure phrases, which join to form eight-measure lines, which join to form 16-measure verses, which join to form 32-bar songs. If a song manages to escape this simple binary pattern, it's usually because something's been added or something's been taken away. That something is usually significant. These ten measures harmonize the lyrics: "You weren't your mama's only son / But her favorite one it seems / She began to cry when you said good-bye / And sank into your dreams."

The words *good-bye* and *dreams* have been lengthened to turn eight measures into ten. Up to this point, the last note of each two-bar phrase (*clean, kerosene, seems*) was about three beats long. *Good-bye* lasts for four beats, followed by four beats of rest. *Dreams* lasts a full eight beats. At first, *good-bye* seems to be the end of the verse, but it comes too soon. The lyric is suspended for a moment before we get the payoff line that sums up the whole song in five words: "and sank into your dreams." This payoff is underscored by the gentle, evocative IV–vi (F–Am) cadence. This cadence was created by substituting a vi chord (Am) for the expected I chord. I don't think it's reading too much into the harmony to note that IV–I is known as the plagal or "amen" cadence used to end hymns. This altered harmony suggests that the person whose dreams are being sung has strayed from the simple solidity of hymns.

This first verse of the song, the only part that addresses "you," is really an introduction. The three main verses, those that deal with the title characters, Pancho and Lefty, are slightly different. The first half of each of these verses follows the same pattern as the introduction:

| I | ⅋ | V | ⅋ |
| IV | ⅋ | I | V |

In the key of C, these chords are:

| C | ⅋ | G | ⅋ |
| F | ⅋ | C | G |

The second half mirrors the second half of the introduction with one beguiling change:

F	⅋	C	F
Am	Dm	⅋ (2 beats)
G	⅋	F	Am	⅋

The ten-bar phrase we saw before is now ten and a half bars with that two-beat bar of Dm inserted in the middle. Van Zandt uses those two beats to extend each line just a little more, giving just that much more emphasis to the last words of the verse.

These two beats of Dm also make an unusual cadence a little more unusual. By placing a Dm between the Am and the G, Van Zandt set us up for a standard vi–ii–V–I cadence

(Am–Dm–G–C). By ending each 18½–measure verse with the vi–IV instead, he kept us a little off balance.

The chorus just repeats that ten-and-a-half–measure pattern. We keep waiting for a more satisfying cadence, but things never quite resolve the way we expect them to. This isn't the playful unevenness of a Dave Brubeck tune like "Take Five" or "Unsquare Dance." This music has a way of getting under your skin, using harmony to make you feel the emotions being described.

In songwriting as in architecture, the most basic structural elements can contribute to the overall aesthetic if you know how to use them. If we were to perform a similar analysis of the lyrics to this song or of its melody, we would find the same subtle balancing of simple, unified elements. We would also find that lyrics, harmony, and melody were themselves carefully balanced with each other to create a unified whole. This is songwriting at its best.

PART THREE

MORE ADVANCED PROGRESSIONS

Music works best when it balances the familiar with the surprising. Write like everyone else and you risk boring your audiences. Be too original and you risk losing them altogether. A good song has enough of the familiar to bring listeners along and enough surprises to make them want to make the trip.

So far, all of the patterns we've discussed have started and ended in the same key—solid, but not surprising. One way to introduce the element of surprise is to move to another key by using *pivot chords*. A pivot chord has one relationship to the chords that precede it and another relationship to the chords that follow it.

Take a look at the beginning chords of Johnny Mercer's "Autumn Leaves," following the pickup measure. (Basic fingerings for the less common chords in this and the other progressions in this chapter are shown at left.)

| Am7 | D7 | Gmaj7 | Cmaj7 | F♯m7♭5 | B7 | Em |

The first four chords constitute a vi–ii–V–I pattern in C major. The last four chords are a VI–ii–V–i pattern in E minor. The Cmaj7 chord that ends one group and begins the next is a pivot chord. It's the I chord in the first phrase and the VI in the second phrase. By playing both roles simultaneously, it links the two phrases together into a longer musical sentence.

Any chord can serve as a pivot chord. In the following example, D minor is both the i chord in a ii–V–i pattern in D minor and the ii chord in a ii–V–I pattern in C major.

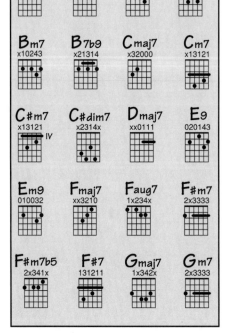

In Dm:		ii	V	i	
	Em	A7	Dm	G7	C
In C:			ii	V	I

The fact that the same chord can play such different roles in different keys means music can be very fluid. Songwriters often exploit this ambiguity to underscore the meaning of their lyrics. For example, what's the key for the first verse of James Taylor's "Don't Let Me Be Lonely Tonight"?

Em9	A13	Dmaj9	B7♭9
Em9	A13	F♯m7	B7
Gmaj7	F♯m7	Bm7	E9
Em9	A13	Dmaj9	B7♭9

Who knows? The first three chords look like a ii–V–I in D. The B7♭9 at the end of the first line, acting as the V of E, leads us back to the Em9 that begins the second line. The ear now thinks that E minor must be the key and hears the A13 and B7 chords as IV and V in that key. The third line gives us a biii–ii–v–I ending on E9, but that E9 doesn't feel very stable. The ear wants it to resolve somewhere. Instead of resolving, Taylor repeats the opening line, futher delaying the resolution. This constant shifting back and forth, toying with our tonal affections, evokes the ambivalence expressed in the lyrics as the singer tells his lover to go away while asking her to stay.

That B7♭9 is an example of a different kind of pivot chord, one created by slightly altering the preceding chord. The notes in a Dmaj7 chord are D, A, C♯, and F♯.

Dmaj7
xx0120

If you change two of those notes by just one fret and add a B in the bass, you get B, D♯, A, C, and F♯.

B7♭9
x21314

The B is optional. You get all the harmonic tension you need to take you back to E minor from just those top four notes. Changing harmonic direction by altering one or more notes in a chord is a wonderfully sneaky way of setting your music off on a new path.

Look at those top four notes again. They form a full diminished-seventh chord, as fine a piece of ambivalence as you're likely to find in tonal music. Technically, the full diminished-seventh chord is the vii7 chord in a harmonic minor scale. But in practical use, any of its four notes can be considered its root. This means you can treat it as the vii7 chord in any of four different keys. You'll remember from our "substitutes for" list that vii substitutes for V. This means that you can substitute a vii7 chord for a V chord and take off in any of four directions.

Taylor takes his vii7 chord in two of those possible directions in the example above: E minor in the second line and G major in the third line. Play and compare those choices to these other two possibilities:

  | Em9 | A13 | Dmaj9 | B7♭9 | C♯m7 |
  | Em9 | A13 | Dmaj9 | B7♭9 | B♭maj7 |

The full diminished-seventh chord isn't the only seventh chord you can ride into new directions. All seventh chords are ambiguous because they all contain more than one chord. This gives us a third kind of pivot chord. Take Cmaj7, for example:

Cmaj7
x32000

If you leave off the bass note C on the fifth string, you've got an E minor chord.

This E minor can be used as a pivot chord between C major and E minor.

In C:	*I*	*IV*	*iii*		
	Cmaj7	Fmaj7	Em	B7	Em
In Em:			*i*	*V*	*i*

It can pivot between C major and D major.

In C:	*I*	*IV*	*iii*		
	Cmaj7	Fmaj7	Em	A7	Dmaj7
In D:			*ii*	*V*	*I*

Or it can take you from C major to G major.

In C:	*I*	*IV*	*iii*			
	Cmaj7	Fmaj7	Em	Am7	D7	Gmaj7
In G:			*vi*	*ii*	*V*	*I*

The top three notes of any seventh chord can be treated as an entirely new chord and take you in new harmonic directions.

MINOR MOVES

You may have noticed that a lot of this tonal ambiguity takes place in minor keys. It's easy to be ambiguous in a minor key. This is because the sixth and seventh notes in minor scales are often raised a half step to create different modes. Chords that include those notes can be diminished, minor, major, or augmented, depending on which mode you're using. There are actually three different minor scales. The chords they produce can be used interchangeably.

In minor keys:

i is minor
ii can be minor or diminished
III can be major or augmented
iv can be minor or major
v can be minor or major
VI can be major or ♯diminished
VII can be major or ♯diminished

The roots of the VI and VII chords can be altered while the other notes in the chords remain the same. This means, for example, that the VI chord in E minor could be C major or C♯dim. The VII chord could be D major or D♯dim.

Take another look at "Autumn Leaves." Mercer chose to build his VI on C rather than C♯. Play both versions of these changes. You'll hear how either could work.

ı Am7 ı D7 ı Gmaj7 ı Cmaj7 ı F♯m7♭5 ı B7 ı Em ı
ı Am7 ı D7 ı Gmaj7 ı C♯dim7 ı F♯m7♭5 ı B7 ı Em ı

All this variety in minor keys offers us one more way of avoiding the expected. If you're tired of using the same old chords in a major key, you can borrow a chord built on the same scale degree in the minor. Take another look at the last two lines of Taylor's "Don't Let Me Be Lonely":

| Gmaj7 | D | Bm7 | E9 |
| Em9 | A13 | Dmaj9 | B7♭9 |

The D–Bm7–E9 progression sounds like it's headed toward A major. Instead, Taylor replaces the E9 with an Em9 and returns to the opening pattern.

In the bebop standard "Cherokee," Ray Noble replaced the major-seventh chords at the end of each line with minor-seventh chords to take us through four keys in 16 measures. Bmaj7 becomes Bm7, Amaj7 becomes Am7, and Gmaj7 becomes Gm7.

C♯m7	F♯7	Bmaj7	⁄
Bm7	E7	Amaj7	⁄
Am7	D7	Gmaj7	⁄
Gm7	C7	Cm7	Faug7

RECAP

Let's take a moment to summarize everything we've discussed about building songs. On the most basic structural level, songs are built on three chords: I, IV, and V.

V goes to I
IV goes to V or I
I goes to IV or V

This basic structure can be altered or extended by substituting other chords for those three basic chords.

ii substitutes for IV
iii or vi substitute for I
vii substitutes for V

Pivot chords can connect short phrases to make longer phrases of songs. There are three kinds of pivot chords: chords that have one relationship to the chords that precede it and another relationship to the chords that follow, chords that are created by altering or dropping one or more notes in a preceding chord, and chords that are borrowed from another mode.

When so many possibilities are laid out before you, it's easy to get bogged down thinking that these are the rules of songwriting. They aren't. They are just precedents created by other songwriters in the past.

None of this would make any sense to you if you couldn't already hear it in your head. Music is a language you already know. You used adjectives long before you knew what an adjective was. Learning these musical terms and techniques will give you a way to explore what you already know, find new ways of writing your own music, and give you a new appreciation of the music you love.

How to Find the Right Guitar

Richard Johnston

Back at the beginning of the '90s, players shopping for a good, affordable acoustic guitar had very few options compared to today. The number of available choices has easily tripled in the intervening years, and the biggest increase is in the number of lower-priced models built by North American manufacturers.

A lot has changed in guitar manufacturing since 1990, and for the most part the consumer comes out the clear winner. The revolution in guitar making, like most other recent changes in our lives, has largely been brought about by the computer. Wherever guitar makers congregate, you'll hear the letters CNC spoken in mantra-like tones. It's no wonder. Computer numerical control has turned the art of lutherie on its centuries-old ear. There's still lots of handwork in building a guitar, but computer-controlled woodworking machinery has brought greater accuracy and efficiency to many stages of the task, and that allows you to get more guitar for less money. Your next car will probably cost a lot more than the one you bought in 1990, but your next guitar doesn't have to.

Along with all that increased efficiency in production has come the ability to produce a wider array of models. The catalogs of major guitar manufacturers are bulging with all sorts of new variations. Once you get into the higher price ranges—say above $2,000 retail—individual guitar makers and small companies offer enticing choices as well. Looking for your next guitar? Great. Want to try as many as possible? Sounds fine, but how many weeks can you take off from work to do it? In the past, the challenge was in finding the right guitar among limited choices; today the burden has shifted to making an educated decision when considering such a large field of instruments offering such incredible variety.

BEFORE YOU SHOP

Now that there are so many more choices out there, how do you go about sorting through them all to find the right guitar for you? Most consumers start by doing their homework. This usually means gathering information about the guitars themselves, but I think that's skipping an important step. Before you start collecting catalogs, browsing Web sites, and studying tonewoods, ask yourself a few questions. Most importantly, it helps to know what, if anything, you *don't* like about your current guitar and what you hope to find in your next instrument. This will help narrow the field of possible choices.

If the guitar you've been playing still sounds pleasing to your ears at least part of the time, maybe you don't want to replace it with another guitar at all. Maybe what you want is an *additional* guitar that is different and gives you some new options in tone. Some shoppers who are determined to limit themselves to one instrument buy a guitar that is radically different from the one they're tired of, only to find a few days or weeks later that absence has made their heart grow fonder of that old pal they

traded in. Some guitarists can get everything they want out of one guitar, while others feel they need several. If you can afford to keep your first instrument, you'll be able to be a little more radical when choosing a second guitar.

It also helps to have a clear view of your financial limits. Remember that playing guitars that are way out of your price range can be a valuable experience, but indulging your guitar fantasies while seriously shopping for another instrument can throw you off the track. Playing a guitar that has everything you're looking for but will require you to live in your car for a year to pay for it can make it almost impossible to be rational about the guitars you can actually afford. Beware the lure of the unobtainable!

Becoming comfortable playing in front of others should be a big part of your preparation. You may not be able to find a quiet room all to yourself in a music store, and sometimes salespeople insist on hovering. Brush up on a few songs that cover your whole range of playing styles and then practice so you can play them with confidence. This is an important step if you don't already play in public, as it allows you to relax and concentrate on the guitars you are trying out and the sounds they make. Whenever possible, play the guitars you are testing in the store in much the same way you play guitar at home. Bring your own picks, for instance, and if you use a capo, bring it along.

AUDITIONING GUITARS

I've been observing people try out guitars for over 25 years and can usually identify those who are going to have a hard time making a choice. They typically bounce from one type of guitar to another, play different snatches of songs haphazardly, and often change everything but their clothes in the process. "This guitar has a lot more clarity than that other one I just played," they might say after strumming the first guitar and fingerpicking the second. Or they might comment that "the first guitar had a nice mellow tone, but this one sounds harsh," when in fact the difference in tone was caused by their picking the strings of the first guitar up near the end of the fretboard and the strings of the second guitar right near the bridge. The confused customer fails to give his ears any consistent information, making it difficult to reach a satisfying decision. If you stay critically focused, you'll more quickly eliminate the guitars that clearly don't suit you, leaving more time to sort through the potential winners. And if you take the task of choosing a guitar seriously, the salesperson will take *you* more seriously and be of much more help.

The number of guitar body shapes offered today means that you have more choices in finding a comfortable guitar than you do when buying a jacket! Manufacturers have also added several new guitar woods to the mix, and if you haven't shopped for an acoustic guitar in the last few years you're in for a surprise. In the not-so-good old days, you had to choose between dreadnoughts, smaller shapes like grand concerts, and the big jumbos. Except for the occasional use of koa and maple, your choices were between rosewood and mahogany for the backs and sides, and the guitar's top was almost always Sitka spruce. Although those choices still represent the majority of steel-string guitars sold, there are now an almost infinite number of variations. Cedar and Engelmann spruce tops are far more common than they were a decade ago, and woods like walnut, ovangkol, and cherry are frequently used for the backs and sides of medium-priced guitars.

We all know that different guitar shapes yield different volume and tone, and we know the woods a guitar is made of also result in a wide variety of sounds. But when you combine those two variables and then try to sort out the results logically, you're courting a cerebral meltdown. Will a dreadnought with a spruce top and walnut back and sides sound brighter than a smaller model of rosewood and cedar? Will that be true regardless of which manufacturer made the guitars being compared? What if one guitar expert or luthier describes the tone produced by a particular wood differently than the manufacturer of the guitar you're interested in? Forget the picks, but please, do you have any aspirin?

Modern guitar manufacturing has produced a bonanza of variety, but there is some question as to whether the end result has significantly expanded the range of guitar sounds. In most cases, the proliferation of new models is simply cutting the same sonic pie into smaller and smaller pieces. I know most guitar makers are going to hate to see this in print, but I think today's guitarists may be better off ignoring all the blather about tonewoods and body shapes and simply trusting their hands, their ears, and their gut reaction to how an instrument looks.

Most people shopping for a guitar will tell you that it's the sound that counts, repeating the old "I'm a player, not a collector" phrase and often embellishing it with admonishments about the folly of those who choose instruments based on appearance alone. Yet very few people ignore what a guitar looks like, despite the rhetoric. And why should they? Believe it or not, most players who choose highly decorated guitars don't spend the extra money just to show off, but rather to please their aesthetic sense. Some people prefer their jewelry with six strings on it. Don't be afraid to state your preferences and stick to them. It's OK to choose the best-sounding guitar from a group of instruments that all have the visual appeal you need. You can't really count on an unattractive guitar's appearance growing on you no matter how good it sounds.

Of course there are people who go to the opposite extreme and sit in a room blindfolded while someone hands them guitars so they can choose one based solely on sound. Despite the purity of purpose such people demonstrate, the cold fact is that most of us don't play instruments as often if we aren't attracted to them, and you usually have to look at a guitar before you get it in your lap and start playing. But do be aware when your visual attraction takes you outside the boundaries of what you need. A pearl-encrusted guitar with a neck that's too big for your hand might look good on the wall, but it will rarely leave that spot.

Another common pitfall is choosing a guitar primarily because it is easy to play. Unless there is something wrong with it, a guitar that feels difficult to play can be adjusted to play more easily, and the one that plays like a dream might only be impressive because it's equipped with lighter strings. Ask what gauge strings are on the guitars you are testing if there seem to be dramatic differences in playability. If the salespeople seem vague about the question, you might want to invest a few bucks in a micrometer so you can be certain that you're testing guitars under equal conditions. Hopefully, the guitar that feels easiest to play offers you the real advantage of a neck that gives your hand a better biomechanical advantage.

BRAND NAMES

If choosing between several body shapes and woods seems daunting, things can get really tricky when it comes to choosing between manufacturers. Different makers produce instruments that look similar but often sound quite different. If you wish to avoid a lot of misinformation, consider these hints:

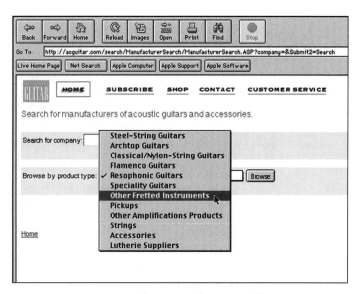

The manufacturer directory at www.acousticguitar.com provides information and links for hundreds of companies.

1. Don't ask music store personnel what they think about a brand they don't carry. There would obviously be a conflict of interest.
2. Be aware that well-meaning friends will try to convince you to share their preference for a particular brand of guitar. It's like getting someone to join their club.
3. Take information from on-line chat groups and user groups with large doses of skepticism. It's easy to pose as an expert when you aren't using your real name. Some people have axes to grind about particular guitar manufacturers, and others just make a hobby of trashing well-known brands.
4. Be open-minded about trying guitar models and brands you haven't heard of, but don't let salespeople divert you from trying the guitars that are high on your wish list.
5. Don't buy based on the warranty. Many warranties are like a politician's promise: they're only good until they're really needed. If you're skeptical about a warranty, call the phone number the manufacture lists and find out what kind of 1-800-TIL HELL FREEZES awaits you on the other end. The retailer you are buying from is often your best advocate in getting decent warranty service.

USED GUITARS

What about new guitars versus used ones? It is beyond the scope of this chapter to guide you through what to look for and what to avoid when buying a used acoustic guitar. However, the time has probably never been better for buying a good, used guitar and saving money when compared to the cost of a comparable new one. The reason for this is simply that major manufacturers have all dramatically increased their production as the acoustic guitar's popularity recovered from its early 1980s slump. That means there are a lot more five-year-old, major-brand guitars in the world than there were ten years ago. As manufacturers continue to load the market with new models, a lot of older models are dislodged from players' homes and sent back to the market to be resold. Many of these instruments have not had much use and are in like-new condition.

Of course, you won't have the wide range of choices when shopping for a used guitar, and you won't have the protection of the manufacturer's warranty, which usually expires when the guitar leaves the hands of its original owner. This means you have to be more knowledgeable about the potential costs of guitar repair. That used model you saw that is selling for $500 less than the best price you've found for a comparable new one isn't a bargain at all after you've had it refretted and had the cracked bridge replaced. Learn how to detect severely worn frets, shallow neck angles, heat damage, and other common problems that may require repair before a used guitar can function like a new one. Here again, your trust in the retailer selling the used guitar can make the difference between a pleasant experience that saves you money and an expensive nightmare that sends you back to playing washtub bass.

BUILT-IN ELECTRONICS

One of the biggest differences in shopping for acoustic guitars in recent years is the manufacturers' increasing use of pickups with on-board electronics in fairly expensive models built of solid woods. Back in 1990, makers would rarely cut big holes in the sides of their guitars for tone and volume controls. If you really use, or plan to use, such an elaborate system, you should consider such a model, but don't feel pressured into buying the guitar of your dreams with extra hardware you don't want. Acoustic guitars have a long life span, and designs have changed only slightly over the decades. Acoustic guitar amplification, on the other hand, is dramatically changing all the time. Today's state-of-the-art pickup system may be tomorrow's equivalent of a black-and-white TV. A guitar manufactured with such a system might turn out to be worth less in the future than a guitar with no pickup at all. If you love the model but don't want on-board electronics, order the guitar without it. You can always add a pickup system later if you really need it, but a hole in the side of the guitar right under your nose is there forever.

THE FINAL DECISION

Once you've waded through the new or used guitars that don't appeal to you, it's time to get more critical of the ones that do. It's easy to become so enamored of the appearance or tone of a guitar that you fail to notice things about it that will really bug you in the long run. Is the neck shape comfortable in your hand? Can you sit in your favorite guitar-playing position and be comfortable? Don't be afraid to ask questions or to ask to see catalogs. If a guitar has everything you like but the neck feels too narrow, for instance, the manufacturer may offer the option of ordering the same guitar but with a neck more suitable for you. Beware of salespeople who continually try to guide you back to purchasing a guitar they have in stock, as that is often the sign of someone who is more interested in a sales commission than in helping you find the right guitar.

It's best to try to ignore the lure of guitars on sale, unless of course they really appeal to you even if you ignore the price tag. A guitar that is heavily discounted may be a great deal, but it can just as easily indicate that it was previously overpriced. In today's fiercely competitive retail market, some manufacturers have resorted to boosting the list prices of their instruments in relation to the store's cost, making the discount percentage impressive to the uninformed but quite meaningless to everyone else. A few months after the purchase, those numbers will be of little comfort if you got a killer deal on a guitar that doesn't suit you.

Let's assume that you've played lots of guitars and narrowed the choices down to a few finalists. How do you decide which guitar is the absolute best for you? Many guitarists can become bogged down at this point and wind up being paralyzed by indecision. Believe it or not, you can't make a truly bad choice at this stage. If you've prepared for your guitar shopping experience and stayed focused on weeding out the instruments that aren't suitable, it's time to relax and trust your judgment. The front-runners are all there for good reasons, and you've eliminated the guitars that don't suit you, so feel free to make the final choice based on appearance, price, or even a coin toss. If you're feeling really cavalier, let your significant other make the final choice (it's guaranteed to make him or her more tolerant of your practicing). With all the choices confronting you today, it's impossible to say that only one guitar would suit you. You've done the work; now take your next guitar home and enjoy it.

Recording Yourself While You Write

Stephen Dick

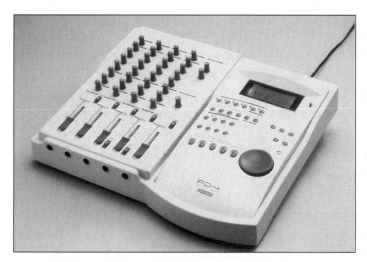 

New digital options: Sony portable DAT and the Fostex FD-4 four-track hard-disk recorder.

I n the British Library, you can see the notebook in which Paul McCartney scribbled the lyrics to "Yesterday." You can stare at it as long as you want, wishing it were more impressive, squinting to see the creative process at work, but it's really just the scribblings of a 20-something kid. In 1965, when "Yesterday" was published, tape recorders were expensive, cumbersome, reel-to-reel monsters and largely out of reach of struggling songwriters. One year later, a product was introduced in Britain and other parts of Europe that would revolutionize the way music was written, rewritten, recorded, and published: the audiocassette.

If vinyl records are the dinosaurs in the evolution of recorded music, then cassettes are the cockroaches, continuing to thrive and flourish as other recording media die off. Cheap, portable, and reusable, cassettes were an instant hit with a generation of young songwriters.

When multitrack cassette recorders came along, a lot of young musicians thought they'd finally arrived in the promised land. At last, a solo songwriter with some multi-instrumental chops could think like a band, laying down parts and bouncing tracks to arrive at a fully developed performance. When MIDI came along, you no longer even had to be able to play an instrument. As long as you were patient, you could shape every note on every instrument one note at a time. With sampling, you didn't even have to do that. You could take the performances of others and, combining them with MIDI loops, layer them into a new creation. When digital multitrack recording came along, the ultimate goal had finally been reached—CD-quality production values within reach of everyone.

So why is it still so hard to write a song as good as "Yesterday"? It's good to remember that a lot of the innovations in home recording over the past 40 years have to do with production, not creation. A songwriter's needs remain pretty basic: a recording environment that stimulates creativity.

CHOOSING A PLATFORM

The recording environment that works best for you is the one that most closely matches the way you create. For example, if you play only instrumental music, you might be better off with a video camera aimed at your left hand while you play. That way, you can catch all those tricky voicings that come naturally when you're improvising but are so hard to remember an hour later.

If you're a great singer but it takes you 20 seconds to go from C to G7 on the guitar, then you might be better off with a setup that allows you to lay in the music separately. This could be a MIDI setup or a multitrack digital recorder.

If you're more of an arranger than a songwriter, layering sounds to build your finished song, then you'll definitely want to use a multitrack setup—anything from the most basic multitrack cassette recorder to a sophisticated digital-audio workstation.

Whatever your chosen setup, be careful not to tie yourself to obsolete or obscure media. A lot of appealing approaches to audio storage have emerged over the past ten years. Some have survived, but most haven't. Musicians alone don't create enough demand to sustain all forms of recording media. Recording formats, whether analog or digital, need a strong consumer demand to survive. The minidisc, for example, is one format that hasn't generated the kind of consumer demand it might have. Will you be able to play your MDs five years from now? Will your repairman be able to get parts to repair your MD player then? Make sure you record your precious thoughts in a medium that's going to be around for a few years.

Whatever setup works for you, it's important not to let recording get in the way of creating. The act of recording your ideas should be as hassle-free as possible. If it's a choice between a state-of-the-art system you have to set up and take down each time you use it versus a portable cassette recorder with a built-in mic, go for the portable. There'll be plenty of time later to lay in all the parts.

SETTING UP

Once you've chosen your basic setup, set aside some time (when you're not trying to record an idea) to find the best setup for clear, clean recordings. Even if you're only using a portable tape recorder, experiment with where to put it to find the best balance between voice and guitar. You'll be amazed at the difference microphone placement can make even at this level. One trick is to place the recorder in the corner of the room where sound reflections from the walls and ceiling can give you a fuller sound.

If your setup allows you to set recording levels, determine the loudest and quietest you normally play and find a level at which you can still capture everything. Don't use reverb or any other effects to sweeten the sound—they can obscure your basic material. Leave these levels and mic positions in place if you can. If you can't, take a picture, do a drawing, put tape on the floor, do whatever you need to do to be able to replicate the setup as quickly as possible.

Also, unless you have perfect pitch, use a tuner to keep your guitar in tune. You'll be amazed at how much easier it is to keep your musical thoughts in order when an E always sounds like an E.

Another basic part of any songwriting setup is simply making sure you have plenty of tape (or whatever recording media you're using) on hand. There's nothing worse than running out of tape when your ideas just won't wait. Also, if you're using cassettes, use shorter tapes, 60 minutes total or less, rather than longer ones. Longer cassette tapes are more prone to distortion.

Don't reuse recording media. Tape is cheap; your ideas are precious. Don't risk losing a great idea by recording over it. Buy media in bulk and use one tape or disc per song or idea rather than trying to cram a dozen half-finished ideas onto one tape.

The most elusive factor in creating a good songwriting environment is habit. Very few serious songwriters can afford to wait for the muse to show up. The creative spark is just too fickle. Most find that having a regular time and place to write, free of distractions, is the only way to ensure continued progress. Five quiet minutes every day is better than a distracted hour grabbed at random.

FINDING YOUR WAY

OK, you've got your quiet place and quiet time. Your levels are set and you've got plenty of tape. Now what?

I wish I could tell you. Everybody writes in his or her own way. What I can tell you is that you should respect your good ideas enough to cultivate them and let them grow. If you've come up with something you thought was good enough to record, you owe it to yourself to look at that idea long enough to discover what made you stop and record it.

Also, don't forget that the whole reason for using a recorder in songwriting is to keep your ideas from getting stale. Storing your flashes of genius is great, but don't just leave them there. The more time that passes after that original flash of inspiration, the more you'll distance yourself from the original idea.

Remember, the original opening words to "Yesterday" were "Scrambled eggs . . . I'm afraid I'm going to lose my legs." Not the strongest poetry Paul ever wrote, but it helped him remember a pretty good tune.

Using a Capo

David Hamburger

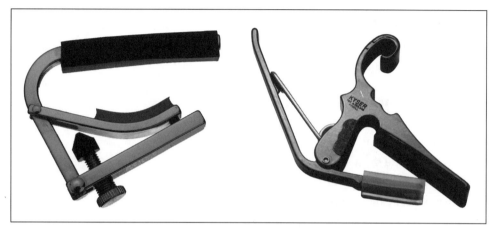

Popular capos from Shubb (left) and kyser.

A capo is designed to raise all six strings of the guitar an equal amount. For example, putting the capo on at the second fret is like tuning every string up one whole step: E becomes F♯, A becomes B, and so on, giving you F♯ B E A C♯ F♯. Now, if you've ever accidentally tuned your low string to the wrong pitch and tuned the rest of the guitar to that, you know that it doesn't matter what pitch the guitar's strings are at, as long as they're all in tune with each other. You can still make all the same chords; they just might not be in tune with everyone else around you. So, if you put the capo at the second fret, you can still form all the same chords. However—and this is an important however—the same chord shapes will now give you, in absolute terms of pitch, all different chords.

ACCOMMODATING YOUR VOICE

The most basic and important use of the capo is to change the key of a song to suit your voice. Let's say you know a song in the key of G with the chords G, C, and D. You've got a great arrangement in G, and you can play the chords in your sleep while you sing the song. The only problem is, G is kind of low for your voice. If you put the capo at the second fret, you can continue to play the same arrangement with all the same fingerings, but it will come out in a higher key. To know what chords you're playing, you'll have to raise the name of each chord by the same amount that you've capoed up the neck. So, if you've capoed up two frets or a whole step, your G-shaped chord is now sounding like an A chord, your C-shaped chord is now yielding a D, and your D-shaped chord is sounding like an E.

If you're trying to raise the key of a tune in E for your voice, you'll be in the key of F if you capo at the first fret and in F♯ at the second fret. Capoing three frets will put you in the key of G, at which point you could remove the capo in favor of using the familiar first-position G, C, and D chords. If your voice feels just right in G♯, you could keep playing E shapes but capo on the fourth fret, or you could use open-G shapes and capo at the first fret.

Here's a chart that shows what chords you get with the five basic open chord shapes as you place the capo on frets one through seven.

Chord Shapes Capoed up the Neck							
No capo	Capo I	II	III	IV	V	VI	VII
C	C♯/D♭	D	D♯/E♭	E	F	F♯/G♭	G
A	A♯/B♭	B	C	C♯/D♭	D	D♯/E♭	E
G	G♯/A♭	A	A♯/B♭	B	C	C♯/D♭	D
E	F	F♯/G♭	G	G♯/A♭	A	A♯/B♭	B
D	D♯/E♭	E	F	F♯/G♭	G	G♯/A♭	A

VARYING CHORD VOICINGS

As you may be realizing, the capo does more than just let you transpose keys. It also lets you begin to make more creative choices about what "key shapes" to use. Each of the standard major open-position keys on the guitar—G, C, E, A, and D—has distinctive qualities and possibilities. To think about our last example again, playing uncapoed in G has a big open sound, which is popular in country and bluegrass music. The chord voicings in the key of E often lend things a more bluesy quality, particularly because the easiest V chord to grab in the key of E is an open B7 chord, which has been used in countless blues guitar arrangements. So by capoing at the third fret and using E chord shapes to play in the key of G, it almost doesn't matter how you pick or strum the song; the chord shapes you've chosen are going to have a substantial impact on the overall effect you create. Keeping this in mind, you can keep a song in the same key while using the capo to allow a certain quality to come through.

Bob Dylan's "Don't Think Twice, It's Alright" is an excellent example of this approach. For years I wondered why Bob made it all the way through this song in the key of E without ever hitting a big fat low E string. For that matter, I wondered why a folkie in 1962 was using things like C♯7 barre chords and why I didn't hear the strings squeak as he moved those barre chords around. Well, it turns out he recorded the tune capoed at the fourth fret so he could get that Mississippi John Hurt sort of sound by using the shapes from the key of C. Capo a C chord up to the fourth fret and it is an E chord, even though in guitaristic terms it still *sounds* like a C chord.

Another example of how a capo can transform a song is the Beatles' "Here Comes the Sun." The song is in the key of A, but rather than playing open A, D, and E chords, George Harrison capos at the seventh fret and uses D shapes. This creates a special kind of shimmer and makes possible the song's distinctive fingerpicking part.

LOWERING THE KEY

You can also use a capo to lower the key. I know that sounds weird, but it's true. Let's return to our I–IV–V song in G (i.e., it uses the chords G, C, and D). Suppose G is too high a key for your voice, but F would be perfect. Well, we all know that playing acoustic guitar in the key of F is about as much fun as being a low-flying pigeon at an Ozzy Osbourne show, so what's the alternative? Try capoing at the third fret and using chord shapes of the key of D. Your D will sound like an F, your G will sound like a B♭, and your A will sound like a C. There you go: F, B♭, and C are the I, IV, and V in the key of F. And best of all, no gnarly barre chords to wrestle with.

B♭ is another key that's hard to play in. If you've written a song in C that's just a bit too high for you, see if you can rework it using G shapes and a capo on the third fret. Your G becomes the B♭, your C becomes the E♭, and your D becomes the F—giving you B♭, E♭, and F, or the I, IV, and V in the key of B♭.

OPEN TUNINGS

Open tunings are another place where the capo can be quite useful. All the great ringing-string sounds and interesting voicings made possible in open tunings completely disappear once you have to start using barre chords. So capos and open tunings really go hand in hand. The capo will let you change keys to suit your voice and will let you use the same tuning for a couple of songs in a row without wearing out the sound of one particular key. In addition, the capo lets you use the same tuning to play bottleneck or slide guitar in more than one key. The way the capo pulls the strings down to the fretboard makes it harder to get a good slide sound than when uncapoed, but slide players from Robert

Johnson to Ry Cooder have made use of the capo to raise open-D tuning up to E or F and open G up to A, B♭, or B.

LEARNING OFF RECORDS

Now that we've looked at the capo from both a practical and a creative point of view, I should point out one more use: investigative tool. As you're trying to figure out guitar parts off of recordings, bear in mind that someone could be using one of the approaches we've talked about here to wax their immortal tracks. Listen for the sound of open strings, and try to identify which chord shapes you're hearing based on your own familiarity with the sound of the five basic shapes—G, C, D, A, and E. Then, if you can't find those sounds on your own guitar in the open position, try to figure out what key the song is in and begin trying various capo positions up the neck.

25 Tunings to Try

Here are 25 alternate tunings—some widely used, some one-off creations of a particular artist—along with song and artist examples. Arrows underneath tuning notes indicate strings that are altered from standard tuning and whether they are tuned up or down. Next to the notes of each tuning, you'll find the chord degree of the open strings. In dropped-D tuning, for example, if you consider D as the root (R), the other strings are the fifth (A), the root again (D), the fourth (G), sixth (B), and second (E) of a D chord, so the tuning is written as R 5 R 4 6 2. Keep in mind that sometimes the artists raise the tuning (and the key) with a capo.

Many of the songs below have been transcribed in *Acoustic Guitar* magazine; for a complete list with tunings and capo positions, searchable by song title, artist, and tuning, go to www.acousticguitar.com. Songs that have appeared in an *Acoustic Guitar* CD Songbook, which include complete transcriptions along with original performances on a compilation CD, are noted with the songbook title in the right column (more details on these can also be found at www.acousticguitar.com). *Acoustic Guitar*'s book *Alternate Tunings Guitar Essentials* includes a more extensive tuning list (60 tunings) along with instruction in various alternate tunings.

Other Web sites that offer valuable tuning information are www.JoniMitchell.com; www.stropes.com, which includes a database of tunings used by Michael Hedges, Leo Kottke, and others; users.plinet.com/~bquade/AlternateTuning102.html, which contains an ingenious, interactive, open-tunings chord guide; and www.harmony-central.com, from which you can download a couple of different alternate-tuning software programs.

SONG	ARTIST	ACOUSTIC GUITAR CD SONGBOOK (See back page)

BASS- AND TREBLE-STRING DROPS

D A D G B E (R 5 R 4 6 2)

Dropped D.

And So It Goes . . .	Steve Tilston	*What Goes Around*
Beeswing	Richard Thompson	
Black Waterside	Bert Jansch	
Coryanna	Stephen Fearing	*Habits of the Heart*
Dust Bowl Children	Peter Rowan	
Embryonic Journey	Jorma Kaukonen	*Fingerstyle Guitar Masterpieces*
Fishing Blues	Taj Mahal	
Green Green Rocky Road	Kate and Anna McGarrigle	*High on a Mountain*
Living in the Country	Pete Seeger	
Look How Far	Bruce Cockburn	
Muir Woods	Andrew York	*High on a Mountain*
Shotgun down the Avalanche	Shawn Colvin	*Shades of Blue*
When You Give It Away	Bruce Cockburn	
Wondering Where the Lions Are	Bruce Cockburn	

E A D G B D (6 2 5 R 3 5)

The Boxer	Paul Simon (intro/lead guitar)	

SONG	ARTIST	ACOUSTIC GUITAR CD SONGBOOK

D A D G B D (R 5 R 5 6 R)

Double dropped D or D modal. Close to standard and frequently used by Neil Young.

Black Queen	Stephen Stills	
Black Water	Doobie Brothers	
Bluebird	Buffalo Springfield	
Free Man in Paris	Joni Mitchell	
Let the Bad Air Out	Bruce Cockburn	
Ohio	Neil Young	
Shelf in the Room	Days of the New	
That House	CPR	*Alternate Tunings Guitar Collection*
Use Me While You Can	Bruce Cockburn	
You Should See the Way	David Wilcox	

D A D G B C (2 6 2 5 7 R)

Galileo	Indigo Girls	
The Moon and St. Christopher	Mary Chapin Carpenter	*Alternate Tunings Guitar Collection*

D TUNINGS

D A D G A D (R 5 R 4 5 R)

Usually referred to by its pronunciation (dad-gad), this tuning is like open D but with a suspended fourth (G) on the third string. This characterizes it as neither major nor minor. It's a favorite tuning of modern fingerstylists and Celtic rhythm guitarists.

After Your Orgasm	David Wilcox	
Barbie	David Wilcox	
Black Mountain Side	Jimmy Page	
Blow 'em Away	David Wilcox	
Catch Me if I Try	David Wilcox	
Ciara	Luka Bloom (C G C F G C)	
Dangerous	David Wilcox	
The Death of Queen Jane	Dáithí Sproule with Trian	*Alternate Tunings Guitar Collection*
Dirt Floor	Chris Whitley (C G C F G C)	
Do I Dare	David Wilcox	
From One Island to Another	Chris Whitley (C♯ G♯ C♯ F♯ G♯ C♯)	
Mary Watches Everything	Luka Bloom	
Spin	David Wilcox	
Strong Chemistry	David Wilcox	
Tango	Patty Larkin	
Western Ridge	David Wilcox (C G C F G C)	
Wild Country	Chris Whitley	

D A D F♯ A D (R 5 R 3 5 R)

Open D. Favored by blues and slide guitarists as well as many folksingers and modern fingerstylists. Sometimes referred to as Vastapol tuning after the song of the same name in open-D tuning. Related tunings: open E, E B E G♯ B E; open C, C G C E G C.

Alive in the World	Jackson Browne	
Amelia	Joni Mitchell (C G C E G C)	

SONG	ARTIST	ACOUSTIC GUITAR CD SONGBOOK
Big Yellow Taxi	Joni Mitchell (E B E G♯ B E)	
Both Sides Now	Joni Mitchell (E B E G♯ B E)	
Center Stage	Indigo Girls	
Chelsea Morning	Joni Mitchell	
Freedom	Richie Havens	
Frozen in the Snow	David Wilcox	
Golden Key	David Wilcox	
If You Love Somebody	Guy Davis (C G C E G C)	Habits of the Heart
Indian Summer	Chris Whitley	
Kindness	David Wilcox	
Little Martha	Allman Brothers (E B E G♯ B E)	
Nothing Ever Lasts	Clive Gregson (C G C E G C)	High on a Mountain
One of These Things	Nick Drake	
Police Dog Blues	Jorma Kaukonen (E B E G♯ B E)	
Prayer in Open D	Emmylou Harris	
Swimming	Pierce Pettis	Acoustic Guitar Artist Songbook, Vol. 1

D A D F A D (R 5 R♭3 5 R)

D minor.

Everything in Its Own Time	Indigo Girls	
Hard Time Killing Floor	Skip James	
John Henry	John Cephas and Phil Wiggins	Alternate Tunings Guitar Collection
Little Hands	Duncan Sheik	

D A D E A D (R 5 R 2 5 R)

A close relative of open D and D A D G A D with a distinctive character from the close interval between the third and fourth strings. Related tunings: E B E F♯ B E.

Days Go By	Duncan Sheik (E B E F♯ B E)	
That's Why I'm Laughing	David Wilcox	

D A C♯ E A E (4 R 3 5 R 5 or R 5 7 2 5 2)

Rainy Road into Atlanta	Cheryl Wheeler	Rhythms of the Road

D A E G A D (R 5 2 4 5 R)

Hejira	Joni Mitchell (B F♯ C♯ E F♯ B)	
My Secret Place	Joni Mitchell (C♯ G♯ D♯ F♯ G♯ C♯)	
Slouching towards Bethlehem	Joni Mitchell	

D A E F♯ A D (R 5 2 3 5 R)

Cherokee Louise	Joni Mitchell	
Deep Lake	Bruce Cockburn (C G D E G C)	
Night Ride Home	Joni Mitchell (C G D E G C)	

SONG	ARTIST	ACOUSTIC GUITAR CD SONGBOOK
Sunny Sunday	Joni Mitchell (C♯ G♯ D♯ E♯ G♯ C♯)	

D A D D A D (R 5 R R 5 R)

Highway in the Wind	Arlo Guthrie
Meditation (Wave upon Wave)	Arlo Guthrie

D D D D A D (R R R R 5 R)

A favorite of Stephen Stills.

4 + 20	Stephen Stills (E E E E B E)
Suite: Judy Blue Eyes	Stephen Stills

G TUNINGS

D G D G B D (5 R 5 R 3 R)

Open G. Probably the most popular tuning for slide guitar. Often called Spanish tuning, referring to the popular open-G song "Spanish Fandango." Also favored by Hawaiian slack-key guitarists, who refer to it as taro-patch tuning. Related tuning: open A, E A E A C♯ E.

Arthur McBride	Paul Brady	*Alternate Tunings Guitar Collection*
The Circle Game	Joni Mitchell	
Daughter	Pearl Jam	
Going to California	Led Zeppelin	
Marcie	Joni Mitchell	
Nightshift	David Wilcox	
Penny for Your Thoughts	Peter Frampton	
Stack Lee's Blues	Steve James	*Rhythms of the Road*
Water Song	Jorma Kaukonen	

D G D G B E (5 R 5 R 3 6)

G6: standard except for the bottom two strings tuned down one whole step.

I Still Want To	Catie Curtis	*What Goes Around*
Hurricanes, Earthquakes, and Tomatoes	Doyle Dykes	*Acoustic Guitar Artist Songbook*, Vol. 1

C TUNINGS

C G D G B E (R 5 2 5 7 3 or 4 R 5 R 3 6)

Low C.

1952 Vincent Black Lightning	Richard Thompson
Just As I Am	Chet Atkins

C G D G B D (R 5 2 5 7 2 or 4 R 5 R 3 5)

Like open-G tuning, but with a nice low C on the bottom. Slack-key guitarists refer to this tuning as C wahine.

Cold Blue Steel and Sweet Fire	Joni Mitchell
Golden Day	David Wilcox
It's Almost Time	David Wilcox

SONG	ARTIST	ACOUSTIC GUITAR CD SONGBOOK

C G C G C E (R 5 R 5 R 3)
ˇ ˇ ˇ ˆ

Open C.

Busted Bicycle	Leo Kottke	
Caledonia	Dougie MacLean	*Alternate Tunings Guitar Collection*
Eye of the Hurricane	David Wilcox	*Alternate Tunings Guitar Collection*
Foxglove	Bruce Cockburn	
Mango	David Wilcox	

C G C G C D (R 5 R 5 R 2)
ˇ ˇ ˇ ˆ ˇ

Altitude	Chris Whitley (C♯ G♯ C♯ G♯ C♯ D♯)	
Carolina	Patty Larkin	
Scrapyard Lullaby	Chris Whitley (C♯ G♯ C♯ G♯ C♯ D♯)	*Habits of the Heart*
Wolf at the Door	Patty Larkin	*What Goes Around*

C G D F C E (R 5 2 4 R 3)
ˇ ˇ ˇ ˆ

A favorite of Joni Mitchell.

Coyote	Joni Mitchell	
Don Juan's Reckless Daughter	Joni Mitchell	
Just Like This Train	Joni Mitchell	
Sistowbell Lane	Joni Mitchell	
Woman of Heart and Mind	Joni Mitchell	

C F C F C F (R 4 R 4 R 4)
ˇ ˇ ˇ ˇ ˆ ˆ

From the Morning	Nick Drake	*High on a Mountain*
Harvest Breed	Nick Drake	

E-MINOR TUNINGS

E B D G A D (R 5 ♭7 ♭3 4 ♭7)
ˆ ˇ ˇ

A favorite tuning of David Crosby.

Déjà Vu	David Crosby	
Guinnevere	David Crosby	

E B B G B D (R 5 5 ♭3 5 ♭7)
ˆ ˇ ˇ

Not a Pretty Girl	Ani DiFranco	*Alternate Tunings Guitar Collection*

MIDDLE-STRING DROPS

E A D G A E (5 R 4 ♭7 R 5 or R 4 ♭7 ♭3 4 R)
ˇ

Caleb Meyer	Gillian Welch	

E A D F♯ B E (R 4 ♭7 2 5 R or 5 R 4 6 2 5)
ˇ

Cello Song	Nick Drake	
The Embers of Eden	Bruce Cockburn	
Isn't That What Friends Are For?	Bruce Cockburn	
Last Night of the World	Bruce Cockburn	
Mango	Bruce Cockburn	*Rhythms of the Road*
The Thoughts of Mary Jane	Nick Drake	

Other Titles from String Letter Publishing

FLATPICKING GUITAR ESSENTIALS

If you love bluegrass and folk music, you'll enjoy using this popular guide to learn flatpicking backup styles, melodies, and leads. The outstanding lessons will inspire you to transcribe bluegrass solos, flatpick fiddle tunes, and add power to your solos.

Book and CD
96 pp., $19.95
Item #21699174
ISBN 1-890490-07-5

ROOTS AND BLUES FINGERSTYLE GUITAR

A treasure trove of traditional American guitar styles by Steve James, one of today's leading roots-music performers, recording artists, and teachers. You'll be inspired and motivated by his clear, accessible arrangements and stories of such masters as Furry Lewis, Sam McGee, and Mance Lipscomb.

Book and CD
96 pp., $19.95
Item #21699214
ISBN 1-890490-14-8

ACOUSTIC GUITAR LEAD AND MELODY BASICS

The experts at *Acoustic Guitar* teach the fundamentals of playing leads in a variety of styles, so players can make a smooth transition from accompanist to soloist.

Book and CD
64 pp., $14.95
Item #21695492
ISBN 1-890490-19-9

ACOUSTIC GUITAR ACCOMPANIMENT BASICS

For beginners as well as seasoned players looking to brush up on the basics, this in-depth CD lesson book provides the essentials of acoustic guitar accompaniment utilizing both fingerpicking and flatpicking techniques in a number of roots styles.

Book and CD
64 pp., $14.95
Item #21695430
ISBN 1-890490-11-3

FINGERSTYLE GUITAR ESSENTIALS

Learn fingerstyle techniques, tunings, and arranging from some of the finest teachers around. This practical guide is packed with tips on fingerstyle accompaniment, arranging for solo guitar, single-note licks and double-stops, and playing 12-bar blues.

Book and CD
96 pp., $19.95
Item #21699145
ISBN 1-890490-06-7

ACOUSTIC BLUES GUITAR ESSENTIALS

Expand your repertoire with this engaging collection of ten great lessons on blues lead, fingerpicking, and slide techniques. Includes six full songs to play.

Book and CD
80 pp., $19.95
Item #21699186
ISBN 1-890490-10-5

CLASSICAL GUITAR ANSWER BOOK

In this expanded edition, Sharon Isbin, virtuoso guitarist and head of the Juilliard School Guitar Department, answers 50 essential questions about performing, practicing, choosing, and caring for your guitar. An absolute must for every classical guitar player.

84 pp. $14.95
Item #21330443
ISBN 1-890490-08-3

SWING GUITAR ESSENTIALS

An introduction to diverse swing styles, pioneering players, and must-hear recordings. Learn movable jazz chords you can apply to hundreds of songs, swinging soloing techniques, jazz melody basics to use in your own arrangements, and lots more.

Book and CD
80 pp., $19.95
Item #21699193
ISBN 1-890490-18-0

ALTERNATE TUNINGS GUITAR ESSENTIALS

Unlocks the secrets of playing and composing in alternate tunings. Included are an introduction to alternate tunings and the players who've pioneered them, in-depth lessons in ten tunings, a special section on how to create custom tunings, and an extensive list of 60 tunings to try, with artist and song examples.

Book and CD
80 pp., $19.95
Item #21695557
ISBN 1-890490-24-5

PERFORMING ACOUSTIC MUSIC

What every performer should know before going on stage. Whether you're a solo performer or a member of a band, stepping on stage for the first time or already building a career, gigging for money or just for the thrill of it, this is the one complete guide to the art of successfully bringing your songs and music to live audiences.

104 pp., $14.95
Item #21695512
ISBN 1-890490-22-9

ACOUSTIC GUITAR OWNER'S MANUAL

We predict that some day all new guitars will come equipped with a copy of this book. Become a more savvy acoustic guitar owner and repair-shop customer. You've made a big investment in your instrument and deserve to know how it works, how to maintain its value, and how to keep it sounding great.

112 pp., $17.95
Item #21330532
ISBN 1-890490-21-0